KILLER VISUAL STRATEGIES

Engage Any Audience,
Improve Comprehension,
and Get Amazing Results
Using Visual Communication

Published by John Wiley & Sons, Inc., Hoboken, New Jersey.

Published simultaneously in Canada.

For general information on our other products and services or for technical support, please contact our Customer Care Department within the United States at (800) 762-2974, outside the United States at (317) 572-3993 or fax (317) 572-4002.

Wiley publishes in a variety of print and electronic formats and by print-on-demand. Some material included with standard print versions of this book may not be included in e-books or in print-on-demand. If this book refers to media such as a CD or DVD that is not included in the version you purchased, you may download this material at http://booksupport.wiley.com. For more information about Wiley products, visit www.wiley.com.

Library of Congress Cataloging-in-Publication Data is Available:

ISBN 9781119680222 (Paperback)

ISBN 9781119680321 (ePDF)

ISBN 9781119680260 (ePub)

Cover and Interior Design: Killer Visual Strategies

Cover Illustration: Killer Visual Strategies

Author Photo: Jennifer Findlay

Printed in the United States of America

V10018675_052620

KILLER VISUAL STRATEGIES

Engage Any Audience,
Improve Comprehension,
and Get Amazing Results
Using Visual Communication

Amy Balliett

Foreword by Guy Kawasaki

WILEY

TABLE OF CONTENTS

FOREWORD

Figure F.1 [ ]

I first came across Killer Visual Strategies, the visual communication agency founded by Amy Balliett, in 2011. That year represented a critical juncture—not just for the fledgling Seattle company, which was just getting their footing in the market, but in the history of visual communication. Smartphone usage was rapidly expanding. A social media platform called Instagram was fresh on the scene. More and more of our information came from nontraditional sources like Facebook and YouTube. And the content we were sharing was overwhelmingly visual.

Amy had launched her company, then called Killer Infographics, to meet a fast-growing demand for infographics from organizations in just about every industry. In fact, Killer first came to my attention when they designed an infographic—now a classic in marketing circles—that pitted me against fellow marketing guru Seth Godin in a tongue-in-cheek standoff (Figures F.1 and F.2). The way in which this and other pieces of visual content—including a motion graphic adaptation of the infographic in 2012—spread virally across the web piqued my interest. These new types of visual content were perfectly suited for posting and sharing on emerging platforms. And people were engaging with them much more than they were with text.

Our world is transforming faster than ever, and visual communication is at the heart of that transformation. Ever since I worked for Steve Jobs as an evangelist for Macintosh, and later for Apple, I knew that good design was fundamental to business success. It wasn't just about the words we used—it was about how we told our story as a company. And that story was about envisioning a better future—with an emphasis on "vision."

For any individual or company looking to make a real difference, storytelling is not just powerful—it's essential. In my career as a venture capitalist, I've heard more pitches than I can count that used hot-button words and jargon, but failed to really deliver a sense of the company's value. To succeed, every organization needs to focus on their purpose, not their product. They must be clear on how they will contribute to a better, brighter future. And communicating that purpose requires visual storytelling.

That's why, in 2014, I became the chief evangelist of Canva, an online service whose goal was to make graphic design easy for people without access to a dedicated design team. Visual content has become intrinsic to how we all communicate, and I knew there was potential in a company that could facilitate such communication. As it turns out, I was right—demand for visual content from consumers and brands alike seems to be growing exponentially. We now expect brands to communicate visually; anything less is not enough.

Today's marketing is therefore visual by necessity. Quality visual communication—from motion graphics to interactive experiences to social-media micronarratives—is no longer an option for brands. Whether you're taking a photo of your office,

preparing a pitch deck for investors, or designing an ebook, you're putting content out in the world that represents your brand. And it needs to represent your brand well.

Visual content doesn't just offer a way for you to build brand recognition. High-quality content will demonstrate your company's commitment to delivering real value. And, perhaps most importantly, the right visual identity for your business will empower you to tell your story in a way that attracts and retains your audience's attention. Because in the end, no brand will succeed without building meaningful relationships with customers and potential customers. Visual communication shows them how their story aligns with yours and envisions what you can accomplish together.

More and more, I'm seeing brands embrace visual content in their internal communication efforts as well. From video training and interactive professional-development modules to company newsletters and boardroom presentations, visual content is driving meaning-making in every aspect of our lives. Branding, meanwhile, is now a company-wide endeavor. Everyone from the CEO to the summer intern should know what your brand identity is and why.

A decade after Killer Visual Strategies was founded, this agency remains at the forefront of innovation in visual communication. They produce more types of visual content than I can count, but they offer much more than that. The Killer team specializes in producing visual content that achieves our goals as marketers. After all, visual marketing is only successful when it's on-message, channel-optimized, and audience-centered.

At the helm of this ship, Amy Balliett has become a global leader in visual communication and visual content marketing, and I can think of no book right now that's more relevant to marketers, designers, and brand leaders than the one you hold in your hands. No matter where your story takes you, this book will be a worthy touchstone along the way.

—Guy Kawasaki
Chief Evangelist of Canva

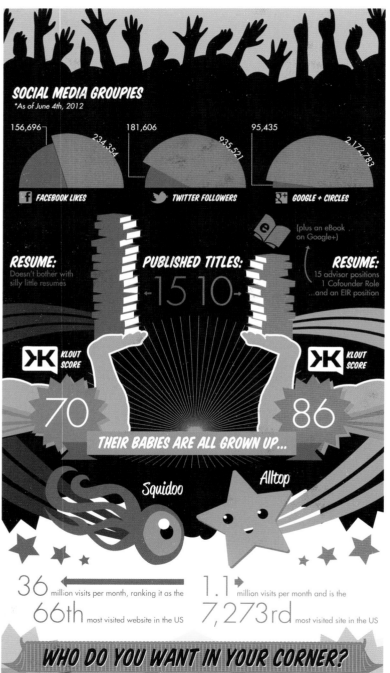

Figure F.2 [ ]

INTRODUCTION

I am not a graphic designer. I am a visual strategist.

This may seem like a small detail, but it's an important one to get out of the way at the onset of this book. Like a food critic who isn't a chef, my skills do not lie in the execution of design, but rather in a unique understanding of how the ingredients of good design come together to create exceptional visual content that is far more palatable than simple eye candy.

While this book will include myriad takeaways for designers, visual communication should be mastered across all avenues of an organization. In fact, this book is made for business professionals of all kinds. It is as much for marketers, brand-builders, educators, and communicators as it is for designers.

This isn't to suggest that designers are not a necessary part of the equation—far from it. If you're like me, and graphic design is not your strong suit, then you'll still need to find a great design partner to fully realize the lessons gleaned from this book.

If you don't have that partner yet, then this book will give you all of the tools and understanding you need to find the right designer or agency partner for your needs. More importantly, it will help you own the outcome of that design work and forge a strong client-vendor partnership to ensure success in the work you do together.

We have entered a world in which 91 percent of today's audiences prefer visual content over any other form of content, according to Demand Gen Report.

This means that anyone charged with communicating information in any organization, whether internally or externally, must rethink how they deliver that information. Visual communication, when properly executed, has the power to greatly increase engagement, comprehension, and follow-through. So if your goal is to meet the visual content demands of your audience, then this book is for you!

With the help of this book, you'll learn how to connect with your target audiences in new and unique ways. You'll gain insights into the shared instincts that subconsciously drive our impressions of brands today. And you'll learn practical strategies to harness the power of visual communication, thus revolutionizing your own content and brand strategy.

You don't need to be a graphic designer to read this book, but when you're done, I hope you will proudly call yourself a visual strategist!

HOW TO READ
THIS BOOK

This book is not meant to be an academic beast of information about the scientific application of visual communication and storytelling. There are dozens of books out there that already fill that need. Instead, this book is actionable. It is written for all levels of understanding with the goal of being easy to digest so that you're empowered to take immediate action within your organization.

This book is broken into three parts, each building on the last without being dependent on it. This means you can start reading at any part of the book; that way, you can gather the information that you find most relevant to your immediate needs. Of course, if you choose to read it cover-to-cover, you'll gain an even more thorough understanding of the subject matter.

THE ACCIDENTAL AGENCY

To lay the foundation for this book, I begin with the story of how my company, Killer Visual Strategies, got started. This story offers a setting for the narrative that follows.

PART 1: VISUAL CONTENT IS KING

To prepare you for the lessons ahead, this section provides critical context that will be applied to the

rules outlined in part 2 of this book. It includes a thorough overview of the environmental factors that have contributed to our present-day consumer demand for visual content by summarizing key moments in recent history that have shifted audience expectations.

Part 1 continues by delivering insights into key elements of audience psychology that inform visual communication today, along with some examples of the varying use cases for visual strategy. This section concludes by exploring the expectations and motivations of audiences today and how this impacts their perception of quality in visual media.

PART 2: 8 RULES OF VISUAL COMMUNICATION

The second part of this book is intended to be both a practical reference guide and a deeper dive into each topic, allowing for either continued reading or immediate application, depending on your needs.

Every chapter in part 2 explains a key rule in visual communication design. You can read these chapters in any order, and do not need to read them all the way through to learn how to apply each rule to your own visual content. Each chapter is broken into three distinct parts that can be read independently of one another or together, depending on how deep you want to delve into the topic. Those parts are as follows:

▸ **Rule:** Each chapter will open with a rule about visual communication followed by a thorough explanation of why the rule exists.

▸ **Exercise:** To best exemplify the rule and put it to the test, an exercise continues the chapter. These exercises do not require knowledge of design software, but from time to time will require you to be near a computer and utilize free online tools.

▸ **Key Takeaways:** To sum up the chapter, I'll share a number of conclusions. If you're short on time, start by reading the key takeaways, which provide concise steps that you can apply to your visual content immediately, along with a summary of the reasoning behind each rule.

You may choose to read just the rules in part 2 and save the exercises for another time. Or you may choose to only read the key takeaways and start applying the lessons to your own content strategy. Ultimately, this section is presented in a way that allows for quick referencing throughout the content development process.

PART 3: YOUR VISUAL STRATEGY

The final narrative section of this book will draw from the lessons in parts 1 and 2 to define a process for developing great visual content. You'll also learn about the different types of teams you can build

to achieve your visual strategy. At the end of each chapter, you'll again find a set of key takeaways. This section is designed to be read from beginning to end to obtain full context, but the key takeaways can also act as easy points of reference for daily use.

APPENDIXES

This book concludes with appendixes comprised of multiple quick-reference materials. You'll find a breakdown of key terms used in visual strategy; tools used for developing great content; production-time estimates for different types of content; and a detailed time line that will take you through the history of visual communication.

Finally, if you ever feel lost, take advantage of the detailed index on the final pages. These will help you find answers quickly so that you can start meeting today's demand for visual content immediately!

> Any images in this book accompanied by this symbol [ ] can be viewed at higher resolution at killervisualstrategies.com/book.

THE ACCIDENTAL AGENCY

> *"It's fine to celebrate success, but it is more important to heed the lessons of failure."*
>
> —*Bill Gates*

In 2010, during the final weeks of June, I designed my first infographic. I had just left the comfort of a six-figure job in marketing for the unpredictable world of startup life. I had worked at startups before, but this was the first time I was truly venturing out on my own with nothing to protect me but a slim safety net of savings.

While my then–business partner and I had been working on launching our business for much of 2009, we had both continued working full-time jobs to keep us afloat. But in June of 2010, I took a leap of faith and quit my day job running search marketing for a directory of colleges. It was the first time that I could realistically dedicate my full attention to our business at the time, an e-commerce software-review service called ZippyCart.com.

ZippyCart was one of many websites we owned, and it was our most successful. We had launched it in 2009 and grown it to a sizeable monthly income as a review and affiliate website. Our goal was to create a handful of other affiliate websites and use content marketing to grow their audience.

I was extremely excited about what was possible within our planned business model. A world of opportunity was in front of me, but financial security—and the peace of mind that came with it—had been thrown out the proverbial window.

I had been the breadwinner of my household. Two years prior, I'd committed to a Seattle mortgage that secured me just 900 square feet of living space for an investment that would have bought me a nine-thousand-square-foot mansion in my hometown of Cleveland. The country was beginning to rebound from the 2008 financial crisis and the cost of living was going nowhere but up. With the weight of the world (or at least my family's financial livelihood) bearing down on me, I needed a disruptive marketing tool that would help grow ZippyCart into a worthwhile brand so that I could provide a reliable income again.

Enter the infographic: the one piece of content that I could not convince my previous employer to even test. I was certain that an infographic would help put ZippyCart on the map, and was willing to bet three crucial weeks of non-revenue-generating productivity on it.

A few weeks later, it was clear that the investment of my time had paid off in spades. The infographic, entitled "The History of E-commerce" (Figure AA.1), delivered more than a thousand inbound links to our website. We moved to page 1 of Google search results for multiple coveted terms, including our target key phrase, "shopping cart reviews." We also saw our PageRank score increase almost overnight.

I was certain that I had mastered a new medium of content marketing, and I was hooked! I quickly jumped at the opportunity to create another infographic, this time on the topic of Google's PageRank methodology. My next infographic (Figure AA.2) took only a weekend for me to produce and led to two thousand inbound links!

I was on cloud nine and nothing could stop me. Infographics were my new secret weapon, so I quickly immersed myself in this burgeoning new world of content strategy.

Figure AA.1 [ ]

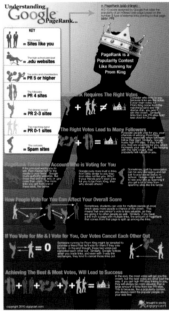

Figure AA.2 [ ]

FIRST LESSON LEARNED: BEING IN THE RIGHT PLACE AT THE RIGHT TIME IS LUCK, NOT SKILL

Fueled by an inflated ego, I began sharing my designs with more experienced entrepreneurs and industry experts. While some chose to remain impartial and offered positive reinforcement, others understood that silence or compliance would only hurt me. One tweet from a business leader I highly respected stood out above the rest and changed everything for me.

Rand Fishkin, founder and CEO of Moz (then SEOMoz), responded to my Google PageRank infographic with four simple words: "That's not an infographic." Nothing more, nothing less.

With those four simple words, I was deflated. What did he mean—my design wasn't an infographic? I had combined images with text and sized the content in the same way other infographics were delivered online. What could I have possibly done wrong?

I considered shrugging off the comment. After all, with thousands of backlinks, I had hard data backing up my success. But Fishkin had made a name for himself by staying ahead of trends and predicting how those trends might impact content marketing best practices. I, on the other hand, had made a living following the advice of Fishkin and people like him. I wanted to dig in and defend myself, but I also wanted to heed the words of someone whose thought leadership had guided much of my marketing career up to that point.

After stepping away and reviewing the infographics (Figures AA.1 and AA.2), it became clear that Fishkin was right. They weren't infographics. If all of the text disappeared from these images, they would no longer make any sense. So how could the graphics possibly be depicting information? And yet, more importantly, how was it that those designs had led to so much success?

The answer, simply put, was that I was in the right place at the right time. Visual content marketing was very new at the time. In fact, from 2008 until early 2012, a marketer could use the word "infographic" to describe almost any piece of visual content and get traction for their efforts. It was because of this that I was stuck in a positive feedback loop—one that had just been throttled by a single tweet.

Fishkin was right. What I had released to the world as "infographics" were anything but. Instead, they were paragraphs of information juxtaposed with imagery that only made sense if you read the text. They were poorly designed and riddled with mistakes, and today they live on multiple lists of the worst infographics of all time!

THE WORST INFOGRAPHICS OF ALL TIME

Now that you've had a moment to look at the "infographics" in question, you likely see what Fishkin saw. If you don't, it's OK. By the end of this book, you'll be able to look at myriad types of visual content and quickly discern what works and what doesn't.

Sometimes you have to learn what not to do before you can truly understand how to change your approach and do things right. Because of this, in future chapters, I will reverse-engineer a number of designs to break down all of the issues within them.

These two designs, for example, taught me a great deal about what not to do when developing a visual communication strategy, while also helping to lay the foundation for the award-winning visual content that I will be sharing in this book. At a high level, here are just a few key takeaways I gleaned from my first two projects:

▸ **Great visual communication relies on tools like Adobe Illustrator.** For my first two projects, I relied on Adobe Photoshop because it was a tool I felt more comfortable with. Illustrator would have been a far better choice due to its agility and robust toolset. More on this later, but for now it's important to note that Photoshop should be used to color-correct and adjust *photos,* just like its name implies.

▸ **A reading assignment is not an infographic.** If you have to read the text to understand the visuals, it's not true visual communication.

▸ **Stock imagery is not the answer.** Great visual communication relies on a skilled illustrator creating custom design, not a mix of stock illustrations and imagery.

▸ **A strict process should be followed to create great visual content.** Without one, you cannot predict timelines, let goals guide decisions, or deliver a narrative that speaks to your target audience.

▸ **Great visual content takes time—but not forever.** One weekend and three weeks are both incorrect timelines to develop this type of content.

These points, and more, will be explained in-depth in part 2 of this book.

MOVING FROM BAD TO KILLER

So how did I go from developing bad infographics for a completely different business to building one of the country's leading visual communication agencies? Partly by accident, to be honest.

Within a month of my Google PageRank infographic, ZippyCart was still benefiting from the associated marketing campaign. If this was the success of a bad design, what could happen with a good one? My business partner at the time was wondering the same thing. In fact, he, more than me at the time, saw the power of infographics and wanted to capitalize on them.

It was because of this that, one August morning of that same summer, he came to me with a domain name and an idea. KillerInfographics.com would be the go-to destination for visual content online. The plan was to create a directory of infographics and provide reviews to build credibility into the directory. This site would then bolster our main business model and add to our portfolio of websites.

Having an SEO background, I added another domain to the idea: SubmitInfographics.com. At the time, Google ranked websites higher in their search engine results pages (SERPs) if the domain name matched the keyword query. We found that "submit infographics" was a highly searched phrase and quickly scooped up the domain. Within a few hours, we had a WordPress site up and running, complete with an automated submission tool, and dubbed it "Submit Infographics by Killer Infographics."

Within a few weeks, I had immersed myself in the hundreds of infographics and motion graphics that were submitted to our site. By reviewing a robust and diverse set of visual content, best practices and patterns began to emerge. It was clear that this was an industry begging for guidance and fraught with internal conflicts between the marketers wanting to capitalize on visual content and the designers asked to deliver it.

I realized that Submit Infographics could be more than a directory of designs. We were uniquely positioned to be thought leaders in a new industry, but in order to do so, we would need to build a better brand. With Killer Infographics, we could define standards for infographic design and lead the conversation in visual communication. I knew we were onto something, but I couldn't yet predict how that would manifest into a business.

ENTER KILLER INFOGRAPHICS, THE AGENCY

At the end of September of 2010, I found clarity. In response to a bad review, a Submit Infographics customer emailed us with a challenge. Their sentiment was simple: they felt that we were hiding behind a screen and a review site and needed to get down off our high horse, so to speak. If we thought we could do better, then they wanted us to prove it, so they offered to pay us to design an infographic for their company.

Immediately, I accepted the challenge. The customer provided me with clear research and gave me an opportunity to put my newly identified best practices to the test. I knew I could produce a great design with the foundation they laid for me, even if the money they offered us wasn't much.

The resulting design was such a success that the customer asked if we had the capacity to take on more work. This presented a unique conflict: our business model was not created to take on clients and offer a subjective service. In fact, this direction was the antithesis of what we had set out to do when starting a company. Our goal had been to create content for ourselves, not for clients.

At the same time, however, that original business model was not working out. By pivoting to design services, I was certain we could buy ourselves some time for our other websites to move up in SERPs

and start generating more revenue. As a result, I convinced my business partner that we could do both. My passion for visual communication was only growing. With infographic design, I saw an opportunity that I couldn't walk away from, even at the risk of my business partnership.

We began by hiring freelancers, a practice that is still common among design agencies, but one that we avoid today. (In part 3 of this book, I'll explain the differences between freelance and in-house design and how these options impact your visual content.) But back in 2010, when I was still testing a new business model, starting with freelance designers was ideal.

In the final quarter of 2010, we landed a few more clients and designed fourteen infographics. We moved out of my then–business partner's townhome office and into a commercial space that could squeeze in five desks. We filled the space with writing interns, focusing their attention on ZippyCart, because we still believed that that would remain our core focus.

But during the first quarter of 2011, it became impossible to juggle both. In that quarter alone, we designed nearly 140 infographics! To keep our eye on the original prize, my business partner kept much of his focus on ZippyCart; meanwhile, I switched much of my attention to Killer.

I threw all of my time into Killer's needs, which included account management, project management, research, art direction, and taking on designs when a freelancer fell through. By touching every part of the process, I continued to hone best practices and learn from past mistakes. This, in tandem with valuable insight from our freelancers, helped to inform the foundations of the process we still follow today.

By June of 2011, we had designed nearly four hundred infographics and began making a name for ourselves. A full year had passed since I took the leap of faith that set me in motion to grow my own business. In just twelve short months, the business I had originally planned for was no longer my focus. Instead, I had experienced a fast and reactive pivot into a very unexpected space.

In the coming years, I would change our company name to Killer Visual Strategies (reflecting a suite of expanded offerings), run visual strategy for some of the world's largest brands, and speak at more than 175 conferences around the globe on the subject of visual communication.

But in June of 2011, I wasn't yet aware of how this new venture would change my life. I still felt just as excited as I had a year prior. I had a world of opportunity in front of me, but so much—including my financial stability—hung in the balance. Only one thing was certain: a year of leaning into my mistakes had brought me further than expected, and there was still so much to learn.

This world of opportunity now lies in front of you. In the coming chapters, I'll share a decade's worth of mistakes and the subsequent lessons learned. More importantly, I'll explain how you can apply those lessons and build upon the killer visual strategies that lead the industry today.

PART ONE:
VISUAL CONTENT IS KING

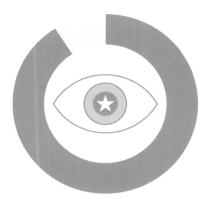

91%

of buyers prefer visual
content to any other form
of content

Figure P1.1
Source: Demand Gen Report.

What fuels widespread consumer demand? Is it driven by environmental factors such as trends and new platforms, or by a subconscious and innate need for the end product?

We live in a world where technological advancements have drastically altered consumer expectations, but it would be risky to ignore how our natural expectations have informed the evolution of these technologies. The power and influence of visual content today offers a perfect example of how these forces work in tandem: as a result of modern platforms in combination with our own fundamental instincts, we are driven to communicate visually more than ever before.

Is the rise of today's visual communication era guided primarily by our surroundings and learned actions, or is it fueled by a set of inherent behaviors? In the chapters that follow, you'll learn about the historical, environmental, and inherent factors contributing to our visual communication–driven world.

In the pages that follow, we'll learn how the demand for visual content grew in tandem with the emergence of new technologies and new ways to connect. Then we'll explore how both our nurtured and natural inclinations have pushed us toward a visually inclined world.

Understanding how nature and nurture work together to engage viewers will not only prove why visual content is truly king when combined with an understanding of perceived quality in design, it will provide you with a universal set of motivators to apply to any audience.

CHAPTER 1
ENVIRONMENTAL INFLUENCES AND THE RISE OF VISUAL CONTENT

"Content is where I expect much of the real money will be made on the Internet, just as it was in broadcasting."

—*Bill Gates*
"Content Is King," (1996)

In 1996, with the dot-com boom in its infancy, Bill Gates published an essay on Microsoft's website that delivered a game-changing prediction for the future of the internet. In that essay, he surmised that "societies will see intense competition—and ample failure as well as success—in all categories of popular content—not just software and news, but also games, entertainment, sports programming, directories, classified advertising, and on-line communities devoted to major interests."

Entitled "Content Is King," this short, yet poignant essay quickly entered the vernacular of brand leaders and marketers looking to capitalize on an exciting new technology called the World Wide Web. Organizations everywhere saw the internet as a new frontier of possibilities, but many were equally apprehensive about the future it held. With his essay, Gates was offering a guiding light: a controllable solution for tackling the unknown. Simply put, to find success online, a brand would simply need to focus its efforts on creating great content.

Of course, anything that seems simple in theory is often more complex in practice. In the world of content, this was and still is quite true.

At the time, the general user would connect to the internet using a dial-up modem and consumer-friendly tools such as Netscape Navigator, AOL, and Prodigy. All of these controlled access to content by leading with their own carefully curated experiences first. There were only so many points of entry for logging on to the internet. Meanwhile, the big players online were not time-tested brands; instead, they were new names that had centered their business around chat rooms and connecting people to each other, rather than to information.

What defined great content was still up for debate, and would be for many years to follow. Advancements in technology would continue to shift what was possible, but in 1996, most content had to be text-based in order to load quickly and remain consumable.

Gates acknowledged this while also predicting future demands as technology improved. In a key takeaway, he noted that "if people are to be expected to put up with turning on a computer to read a screen, they must be rewarded with deep and extremely up-to-date information that they can explore at will. They need to have audio, and *possibly* video. They need an opportunity for personal involvement that goes far beyond that offered through the letters-to-the-editor pages of print magazines."

Surprisingly, he saw one of the largest barriers to success as the computer screen itself. As with most new technologies entering the market, audiences were wary and set in their ways. Information was consumed in print, not in a digital format. To change consumer habits and ensure they would "*put up* with turning on a computer" (italics mine), brands would have to offer creative and wholly unique ways to consume content.

In the years that followed, the mantra that "content is king" would come to define how brands connected with customers online. As demand grew, the need to bring order to chaos drove further innovation.

The concept of blogging saw refinement with sites like OpenDiary (1998), LiveJournal (1999), and Blogger (1999). Suddenly, anyone could share their stories online without a knowledge of code.

The explosion of online content would fuel the foundation of Google, a game-changing search algorithm created by two Stanford University students trying to build a better mousetrap than the Ask Jeeveses and Yahoos of the world.

The internet would set the stage for the rise and fall of myriad companies trying to win the attention of consumers around the world, but Gates's prediction continued to ring true: those that centered their business around accessing, consuming, or sharing content were the ones that remained after the dot-com bubble burst in the early 2000s.

Key Takeaway In the early days of the internet, digital content was restricted by technology. Brand marketers had to rely on text because high-resolution visual media wouldn't load fast enough for viewers. Connecting with audiences by leading with text worked because there were no alternatives, not because it was audiences' preferred medium.

ENTER A NEW MILLENNIUM AND THE RISING DEMAND FOR *VISUAL* CONTENT

Despite the trepidation of many brands reeling from the dot-com bust, the technological innovations that came out of the first decade of the new millennium ignited a content revolution. Sites such as SixDegrees.com and LiveJournal had already introduced the world to the concept of social networking, but Friendster's launch in 2002 combined all the right ingredients to fuel widespread consumer adoption of this concept.

Myspace, LinkedIn, and numerous other players entered the space shortly after, and the social media arms race began. Each site worked to differentiate itself. LinkedIn focused on remaining niche and topical, centering its branding and content around career connections and mobility. Myspace and Friendster, on the other hand, hoped to cast a far wider net.

Both channels strove to deliver the best user experience for eager audiences hoping to find a home for their online personalities. Popular features tapped in to user vanity, offering the ability to see who viewed your profile or sort a friends list by top friends.

The opportunity to express oneself through design was one of the greatest draws of Friendster and Myspace. Users would spend hours picking the best wallpaper background or choosing their preferred fonts and colors. Eager upstarts jumped at the opportunity to make this customization process even easier and centered their businesses around the two platforms. Anyone looking to show off a new style could purchase wallpapers online or pay for bespoke designs from a variety of DIY and white-glove services.

In tandem with the rise of social media, the ability to create multimedia content became easier than ever before. Film was on the move to digital, camera-ready cell phones sat in the pockets of consumers everywhere, and YouTube revolutionized home video for a new generation.

To keep up with demand, both Myspace and Friendster continued to introduce multimedia content to their platforms. The ability to share photos and video was no longer just nice to have, it was necessary for maintaining their user bases. The internet was a powerful tool for building connections, and viewers were inclined to share user-generated visual content above all else.

By 2006, Myspace had become the most popular social network on the web, but all eyes were on a quiet upstart that had already circulated widely through college campuses. Facebook delivered an experience that made sharing photos and video easy, but with a minimalist aesthetic that did not offer highly customizable profile pages to express oneself. While some saw this as a drawback, this subtle differentiator may have been one of Facebook's more attractive features. Friendster was struggling to keep users coming back, while Myspace was losing its appeal for many. Pages felt loud, cluttered, and obnoxious to viewers, and lacked credibility as a result. Facebook's clean look and feel still offered a quality user experience, but delivered content in a uniform package.

In the autumn of 2006, Facebook opened its doors to anyone thirteen years or older. This social network, once exclusive to college students, was now attempting to usurp Myspace and Friendster.

Key Takeaway Advancements in mobile camera technology and the advent of social media worked in tandem to shift consumer behavior and expectations. This was just the beginning of our modern relationship with visual media. Thanks to these innovations, visual content became easier to create and grew to be an integral part of our online identities.

2007: THE YEAR THAT CHANGED EVERYTHING

Renowned author and thought leader Malcolm Gladwell defines a tipping point as "the moment of critical mass, the threshold, the boiling point." It can be argued that 2007 was one of the most pivotal years in content and the tipping point that gave rise to today's visually driven consumer audience.

The year began with one of the most notable innovations of our time. It was January and everyone was excited to hear a new announcement from Apple cofounder and CEO Steve Jobs. He walked out onto the stage at the Macworld conference in his signature black turtleneck and, in an instant, changed how we consume content forever.

The iPhone, which Jobs premiered that day in San Francisco, would reinvent media for a new generation. While in 1996 Gates was concerned with compelling users to simply turn on their computers and give their attention to a screen, a decade later Jobs was so confident that screens would drive connections that he made them pocket-sized for immediate access.

Suddenly, a tool for finding and sharing content was at everyone's fingertips. Anyone with an iPhone could immerse themselves in videos, photography, social media, and more. The iPhone killed Adobe's Flash, forced brands to consider responsive design, and taught audiences to expect content that could communicate large-scale information in a pocket-sized viewing window.

This shift boded well for Facebook, whose newsfeed offered an optimal experience for anyone connecting via their phone. A large influx of users moved to the social network that year; in fact, according to the Associated Press, Facebook's active user base grew from twelve million at the end of 2006 to twenty million by the next April, then to a whopping fifty million by October 2007 (Figure 1.1)! Myspace—which at one point controlled 80 percent of social media traffic online, according to Elise Moreau in *Lifewire*—still had more users, but the growth trajectory was clear. Facebook was going nowhere but up, and along the way, it was retraining viewers to consume and share information beyond the profile page.

In the spring of 2007, another big shift in communication took place. Twitter, which had launched just a year prior, experienced widespread adoption during the South by Southwest (SXSW) conference in March. Twitter's presence at the conference was perfect timing. People were keen to connect with one another to organize meetups, and the platform was a perfect place to do so. With little effort and in the span of a few days, Twitter quickly jumped to sixty thousand tweets per day, *Lifewire* reports, and suddenly the concept of communicating in short-form text began to take hold.

In sum, 2007 proved to be a banner year for new media and entertainment. The iPhone app store

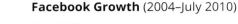

Facebook Growth (2004–July 2010)

1 million — End of 2004

5.5 million — End of 2005

12 million — End of 2006

20 million — April 2007

50 million — October 2007

100 million — August 2008

150 million — January 2009

175 million — February 2009

200 million — April 2009

250 million — July 2009

300 million — September 2009

350 million — End of 2009

400 million — February 2010

500 million — July 2010

Figure 1.1
Source: Associated Press, "Number of Active Users at Facebook over the Years."

delivered new games, easy photo editing and filters, design tools, and communication services beyond anyone's imagination. Brands that had spent years learning how to compete on a computer screen suddenly had new channels at their disposal that

offered unlimited connection points with their customers. The possibilities for marketers seemed endless as consumers' pockets began vibrating with emoticons, tweets, push notifications, and status updates.

But a financial crisis was looming on the horizon, and savvy brands knew they needed to take steps to protect themselves from the fallout. A couple years earlier, some economists had started predicting the impending crisis, but by 2007, reports of a mortgage industry propped up on bad debt were circulating widely. For the first time since rumors of a downfall began, the economic cynics outnumbered the idealists. Large organizations took notice and looked to new trends to remain relevant to their customers while also reducing spending wherever possible.

A perfect storm was brewing. On the one hand, organizations had more opportunities than ever to engage their audience, but on the other hand, with an economy on thin ice, taking advantage of those opportunities would require very careful planning. Many of these channels were new and untested, so organizations often had to navigate uncharted waters while trying to mitigate the risk to their bottom lines.

Luckily, in the eye of the storm there was hope. The internet had connected an entire generation, training young minds to keep up with technological advancements at breakneck speeds. With email, chat tools, and Voice over Internet Protocol (VoIP), communication had no borders. The gig economy, which had been around in one shape or form for decades, began growing faster than ever. Work was no longer confined to a cubicle, which meant that brands could draw on affordable talent from anywhere to accomplish their goals.

Social media offered another important ingredient to lower risk and fortify businesses in the face of an impending crisis. It presented brands with a wealth of data about their audiences that was far greater than any on-site analytics tool could do. And that information was loudly saying one thing: from video and memes to selfies and GIFs, it was clear that consumers loved visual content above all else.

At a time when organizations would be left behind if they didn't establish a presence on multiple channels, visual content offered a safe and innovative way to reinvent their marketing programs. When executed properly, visual content had the power to be small enough to look great on all screen sizes, and engaging enough to disrupt a news feed. What's more, the emerging gig economy would make it very affordable to deliver.

By the end of 2007, the scales of content had tipped, and all trends were pointing toward visual media as the king of kings. Long-form, text-heavy content required lengthy research periods, expert writing, and design. It simply wouldn't do in a world that was growing to expect immediate access to ever-changing information.

Key Takeaway The year 2007 completely changed content expectations, and many organizations are still feeling the impact of this seismic shift. Through understanding the myriad changes that took place during this single year, organizations can better appreciate how advancements in technology should challenge status quo. Pay attention to periods of vast innovation and consider how they will impact your own strategies.

A DECADE DRIVEN BY VISUAL MEDIA

In the decade that followed, consumer audiences' expectations rapidly evolved while attention spans dwindled at the same pace. Emerging platforms online continued to shift the ways in which brands created content and audiences consumed that content. To keep up, brand marketers found themselves creating dozens of pieces of visual content to accomplish singular goals.

The decade saw the rise of freelance job boards that would connect creators from all over the world to brands eager to capitalize on new trends. The international nature of the gig economy meant that talent was competing for work against lower-priced counterparts, and global economic conditions meant organizations favored overseas price points.

To compete, on-shore freelancers would either succumb to downward pricing pressures or would need to find more efficient ways to deliver great content to their clients. This led to a rise in stock vector sites, WordPress themes, and more. Companies such as Adobe and Apple flourished as a result, consistently releasing robust feature sets to help content creators compete while creating a culture of loyal and repeat customers whose livelihoods would come to rely on their products.

Unfortunately, as services rushed to keep up with demand and brands continued to plan budgets around low-cost alternatives, the output was often lower-quality visual content. The fact that subpar designs still saw success (at least in the first half of the decade) further proved the overwhelming consumer preference for visual media. In fact, it seemed that audiences had such a craving for visual content that, for a while at least, there was little concern over how well a design was executed.

Content providers continued to search for ways to make their experiences sticky and shareable. BuzzFeed quickly garnered a following with their focus on listicles and quizzes. This gave traditional news outlets a run for their money as more eyes moved toward these far more engaging content formats. While quizzes catered to ego, listicles catered to dwindling attention spans.

With so much information at the fingertips of the masses, parsing and compartmentalizing long-form content ensured that information would be easy to digest. The listicle, which combined headlines with relevant images, trained viewers to consume content by first viewing headlines and their associated imagery before ever diving into a single paragraph. The listicle wasn't a new form of media, but animated GIFs allowed BuzzFeed to give it a much-needed upgrade for the growing Visual Generation.

The fast-paced and interactive experience of a quiz often led to visually rich, shareable output on social media. This disrupted the news feed and fueled vanity, two factors that, when combined, were perfect ingredients for viral appeal.

By combining pop culture with personality tests, users could share their results in data-driven pie charts and bar graphs. Through simple data visualizations, they could easily compare themselves to the masses and would eagerly announce what made them unique for the world to see.

As smartphones evolved to deliver best-in-class cameras and photo-editing tools, Instagram took the world by storm. At the same time, consumers eagerly organized their lives through imagery on Pinterest which, at one point, drove more business traffic to websites than Google+, YouTube, and LinkedIn combined, according to a 2012 referral traffic report compiled by *Shareaholic*. It wouldn't be long before Snapchat gained an avid user base of people eager to connect via video, filters, and captioned photography. Words like "pin" and "snap" took on entirely new meanings as consumers shifted their habits to embrace a world rich in visual communication.

While audiences were interacting with their phone and computer screens to create and share visual media, they were moving away from the big screen. The financial crisis had already impacted attendance at movie theaters, and now, big-box video stores were disappearing in droves. Consumers turned their attention to streaming services that offered the same convenience and instant gratification that social media and smartphones had taught them to expect.

Visual media in all forms became commonplace to such an extent that it was weaponized during the 2016 US presidential election. Foreign powers, Cambridge Analytica, and political pundits paired unflattering photography of candidates with false quotes and information. Creative video-editing tactics were used to deliver news stories that were wholly inaccurate. Viewers, who had learned to value visual content as a medium for information delivery, willingly trusted what they saw, and the era of fake news became a reality.

In a twenty-year span, the prediction that content would be king proved beyond accurate. Global industries saw extreme success or utter failure based entirely on how fast they could deliver engaging visual media. Political rivals won or lost based on their ability to manipulate and react to it. In every aspect, visual content was no longer just a nice-to-have—it became the single most compelling motivator of the modern era.

Today, the strictly text-based content that drove the predictions of Bill Gates in 1996 no longer applies. Now, visual content is king, and the organizations that don't embrace this reality will likely see the same demise as Digg, Blockbuster, and Borders. Of course, if you've never heard of those brands, then I've made my point.

Key Takeaway The immense demand for visual content is not going away. If anything, it has become a staple of our society, woven into the very fabric of who we are and how we connect with one another. For brands to survive and, ultimately, thrive, they must develop and prioritize visual strategies.

CHAPTER 2
VISUAL CONTENT AND HUMAN NATURE

"The broader one's understanding of the human experience, the better design we will have."

—*Steve Jobs*

While advancements in technology helped fuel the rising demand for visual content, our universal embrace of that content must be considered an equally valid indicator of its power and effectiveness. When organizations were competing for their corner of the internet, the ones that led with visual content saw far more success than those that relied on text-heavy alternatives. In fact, the most successful innovations that followed were often founded on a visual-first mentality.

So what has driven audiences to crave visual content above all else? To answer this question, we have to understand human psychology and our innate predilection toward visual communication.

Scientists, philosophers, and linguists have debated the origin of both verbal and written language for centuries. Did the ability to communicate through a common language occur as a learned social construct, or was it a sudden evolutionary shift wherein our species developed a natural inclination to formulate words from thoughts? This particular debate may never find a true answer, but there is no debate that verbal and especially written language developed long after the earliest humans appeared.

When challenged with the need to communicate, early hunter-gatherers expressed themselves with visual depictions of their message long before the tools for written language became the norm. In other words, visual language first arose as a response to our need to communicate and build connections.

Cave paintings are the first clue to suggest that the human species is hardwired to speak visually. In the same way our own fight-or-flight instincts can be traced back to our ancient ancestors, our bias toward visual expression has remained part of our natural makeup as well.

One of the most exciting ways to witness our inherent need to connect and communicate visually can be seen in the reactions of toddlers turning the pages of picture books. Long before a true understanding of the words on the page can be formed, colors and illustrations demand their attention. We are attracted to visual content even before a written storyline endows illustration with meaning.

Key Takeaway We are naturally inclined to communicate visually. Embracing this element of human nature is imperative to creating a great visual strategy.

THE BRAIN SCIENCE OF VISUAL COMMUNICATION

Brain science suggests that our natural inclination to communicate visually is a dominant human trait. In fact, 30 percent of our cerebral cortex is composed of neurons firing together to drive visual processing, according to

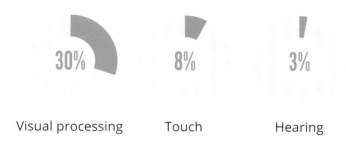

Visual processing   Touch   Hearing

Figure 2.1
Source: Grady, "The Vision Thing."

Discover. When compared with only 8 percent for touch and 3 percent for hearing (see Figure 2.1), this suggests that we prefer visual communication innately.

One of the most notable pieces of evidence for just how integral visual communication is to the human brain comes from a 2005 study called Project Prakash. Led by MIT professor Pawan Sinha, Project Prakash worked with the Shroff Charity Eye Hospital in New Delhi, India, to help restore sight to those who were blind as a result of congenital disease.

According to MIT, 30 percent of the world's entire blind population resides in India. The numbers are so vast because many of those suffering from blindness either lack access to quality health care or lack the financial means to obtain it. According to estimates from the World Health Organization, 60 percent of India's blind children die before they reach adulthood, despite the fact that more than 40 percent of cases are preventable or treatable.

In a seemingly hopeless situation, Professor Sinha saw opportunity. With the help of undergraduate and

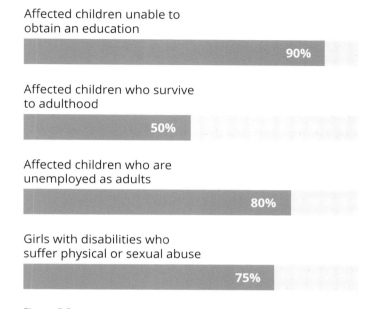

Figure 2.2
Source: Project Prakash.

graduate students at MIT, as well as postdoctoral fellows, Sinha established a presence in India to help cure blindness in more than two thousand patients! Beyond the great humanitarian effort, his work took the scientific understanding of how our brains learn to see to an entirely new level.

From 1981 until Sinha's findings in 2005, the general opinion of the scientific community assumed that the brain could not perform visual processing if sight were restored after six years of age. This theory came from a series of studies performed by scientists David Hubel and Torsten Wiesel in the late 1970s and early '80s. They would later win a Nobel Prize for their work in visual physiology.

Their work surmised that the visual cortex, left unused for a period of time, would do what other parts of the human brain does: rework itself to give more attention to our other senses. This theory is exemplified most iconically in the case of Stan Lee's famed comic hero, Daredevil. This blind protagonist wasn't hindered by his impairment. Instead, his blindness improved all of his other senses, allowing him to best his presumptuous adversaries with ease.

Of course, life is not a comic book, and the brain's visual processing capabilities seemed to Sinha to be far too powerful to simply be overtaken by senses that the brain already gives less priority to. So, Sinha sought to challenge the work of Hubel and Wiesel. He went to India, where he could cure children and adults of long-term blindness while gaining insights into how their brains would rebound, if at all.

What he uncovered challenged more than twenty years of scientific understanding. Not only did every patient regain sight, but even adults who had been blind for decades saw full recovery. In other words, the visual-processing part of our brain is so powerful that, even after years of no sight, the gray matter will wake up and, where needed, repair itself.

In the weeks following restoration of sight, Sinha was able to run a plethora of tests on patients to determine how the brain learns to see. During this time, he learned that our brains process simple shapes before complex imagery. This suggests that elements like simple iconography can connect with the human brain faster than detailed illustrations and photography. He also learned that moving imagery is far easier for the brain to process. This might explain our penchant for television, cinema, video, and motion graphics.

Visual communication is clearly a guiding priority for the human brain. In fact, multiple studies have tried to quantify the brain's visual-processing abilities. The most notable, which was published in the *SAGE Handbook of Political Communication* by Semetko and Scammell in 2012 and has held up ever since, stated that visual information gets to the brain sixty thousand times faster than any other form of communication that exists (Figure 2.3)!

Visuals communicate information faster than words—by one estimate, **60,000x faster**

Figure 2.3
Source: Semetko and Scammell, *The SAGE Handbook of Political Communication.*

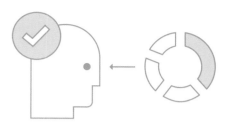

36,000

The number of visual messages
human eyes can register per hour

Figure 2.4
Sources: Jensen, *Brain-Based Learning: The New Paradigm of Teaching*; Brysbaert, "How Many Words Do We
Read per Minute?"

15,000

The number of words the
average adult can read per hour

1 MINUTE OF VIDEO IS
WORTH 1.8 MILLION WORDS

Figure 2.5
Source: McQuivey, "How Video Will Take over the World."

To put this into perspective, the human eye can register 36,000 visual messages in any given hour, reports Dr. Eric Jensen, author of *Brain-Based Learning* (Figure 2.4). In comparison, the average adult can only consume 14,280 words of text in that same hour, according to meta-analysis published by Marc Brysbaert of Ghent University in 2019. With visual content, the brain quickly discerns meaning by creating messages, but with text-based content, the brain must string together words to form sentences that then create meaning. To up the ante even more and give a nod to Sinha's findings, Forrester Research suggests that just one minute of video is worth 1.8 million words (Figure 2.5)!

We are predominantly visual learners as well. As e-learning has become more popular, educators have had to find ways to improve understanding outside of the classroom. They found that combining text with graphics led to an 89 percent increase in comprehension when compared to just delivering text alone, as reported in *e-Learning and the Science of Instruction,* a handbook for e-learning professionals.

Our brains come prepackaged with the toolset to take any information that we consume and convert it into a visual format. To test this, take a moment to ask those around you what they think of when you say a simple word like "dog." You'll notice that, for some, an image of dogs will pop into their heads, while others will think of cats, a bone, and so on. Very few people, if any, will tell you that they thought of the letters d-o-g. In fact, if someone does think of the letters, ask them if they are multilingual. It's often those who have trained their brains to speak across languages that have to process information in this way. This is because we don't instinctively think in text—we instead think visually.

Key Takeaway Not only do we communicate visually, but we think visually as well. When connecting with your audience through text, you are adding an extra step for the brain to process the information you are sharing. By leading with visuals, you have the opportunity to engage your audience far more efficiently.

SPEAKING VISUALLY IS NATURAL—AND NOW, IT'S EXPECTED

The technological advancements of our modern age have placed us all in a constant state of information overload, and we are eager to seek cover from the storm. We crave information, but in order to process it all we yearn for clarity in the noise. Because of this, we have instinctively turned our attention to the easiest-to-digest content media out there: visual media. It's because of this that the brands that deliver successful visual strategies are those that value the innate expectations of their consumers. Those that still lead with text will continue to struggle.

But we are discerning creatures. Just as we can process visual content in an instant, we can judge that content equally as fast. While organizations continue to lead with new media such as infographics, e-books, motion graphics, and more, they have to consider the execution of this content. Just like my first two attempted infographics, simply placing images next to paragraphs of text won't work, because it forces the viewer to read the content to understand the visuals. Instead, to succeed in a world that demands a visual conversation, organizations must lead with true visual communication.

Visual communication graphically represents information to efficiently and effectively create meaning. When needed, limited text is used to explicate that meaning. In other words, your visual choices must speak louder than your text. Your audience is ready to process your visual information, but not if that content makes little sense without the support of text to elevate it.

But how do you deliver content that both takes advantage of our modern platforms and connects with our fundamental instincts? In the second part of this book, I'll explain exactly that.

CHAPTER 3
QUALITY VISUAL CONTENT REIGNS SUPREME

94% OF A BRAND'S FIRST IMPRESSIONS ARE BASED ON DESIGN

Figure 3.1
Source: Sillence et al., "Trust and Mistrust of Online Health Sites."

While visual content in all its forms is king, quality visual content is the monarch that reigns supreme. Our ability to quickly process visual information ensures that we often can't stop ourselves from subconsciously judging a book by its cover. And while opinions of quality may differ from person to person, there are universal expectations that align all audiences that brands must cater to.

The concept that we are all united by a set of aesthetic expectations may be most evident in the ways in which we judge physical attraction. Everyone is unique in what appeals most to them, but audiences often find common ground and form collective opinions on whom we deem handsome or beautiful. While commonly held definitions of beauty are often social and cultural constructs rather than reflections of objective fact, they are nonetheless powerful. This widespread appeal is used by brands of all sizes to garner consumer trust, attention, and ultimately sell us their latest products or services.

We are so attracted to beauty that it can easily cloud our judgement and lead us to unfounded and often unwavering conclusions. This is called the "halo effect," a term that was coined by the psychologist Edward Thorndike in 1920.

In 1915, Thorndike conducted a study among commanding officers in the military asking them to evaluate their subordinate soldiers across a variety of factors. They were to consider leadership, intelligence, loyalty, industry, dependability, and physical appearance as key performance indicators.

For the purpose of ensuring a good sample set, all soldiers had been considered as fairly equal and consistent in their overall performance across these categories on paper. But once their physical appearance factored into the equation, the commanding officers' view of these soldiers greatly changed. A clear correlation was drawn, showing higher ratings across the board for those who were also considered to be physically appealing, while those considered less attractive earned far lower ratings across the board.

Also known as the "what is beautiful is good" principle, the halo effect suggests that people look more favorably upon those who are deemed attractive. In the same vein, more judgement is subconsciously cast upon those who are considered to be less attractive by common standards.

Decades later, studies suggested that human nature had not changed. In a 1974 study performed by psychologists David Landy and Harold Sigall, sixty male undergraduates were asked to judge an essay that they were told was written by a female college student. These undergraduates were broken into groups in which twenty were provided a photo of an ostensibly attractive author, twenty were given a photo of an unattractive author, and the other twenty were not provided a photo of the author at all. Half of the group was then given a seemingly well-written essay while the other half was given an essay in which the objective quality was considered poor.

The results of the study overwhelmingly showed that the content of the essay played less of a role in final evaluations than the writer's supposed attractiveness. In fact, students who perceived that the writer was attractive rated her more favorably than those who did not have insight into her looks. And those who viewed her as unattractive rated the work lower in perceived quality than the others, even when given the same content. This held even more true when reviewing the lower-quality essay, for which the more attractive writer received better reviews, despite the execution of the work itself. This study has been replicated throughout the years, each time leading to the same conclusions.

Brands often take advantage of the halo effect. By using celebrity endorsements and models in tandem with their products, they're subscribing to a formula that inspires seemingly instant trust and engagement among their audiences. But this effect goes beyond how we perceive people. Just as we may share common opinions on physical beauty, we often align in our impressions of design.

Perhaps one of the best ways to exemplify this lies in something as simple as website performance. Websites are a brand's most important content asset. Sites that engage viewers are often visually rich, leading with motion graphics, infographics, iconography, and more to drive users through a conversion funnel.

A study published by Swedish technology researchers Bo N. Schenkman and Fredrik U. Jönsson identified that the overall quality of a website is often judged by four key factors: beauty, use of illustrations over text, broad overview, and site structure. Of these four considerations, the perceived beauty of a website was often the best predictor of positive impressions. In other words, a poorly designed website will greatly hinder the success of the associated brand.

Quality design builds trust with a viewer, whereas something with a jumbled, rushed, or disorganized aesthetic direction often leads a viewer to question the merits of the associated brand. eBay found this to be a problem in 2010. Sellers with great ratings but poorly designed websites saw sales falter, while those that had low ratings but well-designed websites were deemed more trustworthy to purchase from. This might be why alternative auction sites online have been able to compete although eBay originally took the market by storm.

SO: BEAUTIFUL DESIGN REIGNS SUPREME?

You might be wondering why quality design is ultimately more effective than beautiful designs.

Imagine if you had the option of living in one of two houses. From a purely aesthetic perspective, both homes are extremely eye-catching. They incorporate all of the finishes you love in a house, have great curb appeal, and even have that wine cellar you've always wanted. At first glance, you would be thrilled to make your life in either of them.

But there's a reason people learn about the bones of a house prior to buying. What if one of the two houses didn't have working plumbing? What if the foundation was sinking or the walls were not insulated? Suddenly, these two homes that look the same and cost the same no longer deliver the same value for a buyer. While both catch your eye, only one can actually function in the way you need. Your perception of quality between the two homes is now quite different than it was upon first glance.

While this may be an extreme example, delivering value through your content is just as important as delivering something that's visually appealing to the viewer. Of course you can have something that looks beautiful and quickly engages your target audience simply because of the "wow" factor of the design. But to keep their attention and build long-term loyalty, your content has to deliver value beyond a pretty picture. This marriage of form (perceived beauty) and function (perceived value) combine to provide a quality end product.

The concept of balancing form and function in design is nothing new, but it is a key differentiator between simple design and true visual communication. If your sole focus is on making your visual content look good, it's unlikely that it will deliver any relevant information. While audiences may connect with and

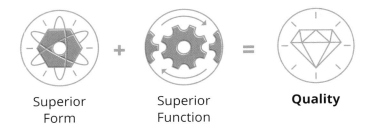

Superior Form + Superior Function = **Quality**

Figure 3.2

even share a beautiful image, if that design doesn't carry forward meaning, it won't inspire action. Just as a poor design will deter most audiences, delivering content that doesn't have an equal focus on function will lead to missed opportunities and minimal engagement.

According to a 2018 report from Adobe and Econsultancy, organizations that lead with a commitment to "design-driven" quality in their content are 69 percent more likely than their competitors to exceed their yearly revenue goals. By delivering content that puts an equal focus on form and function, brands have the opportunity to stand out from the crowd (Figure 3.2).

There is likely no better example of this than Netflix. What began as a mail-delivery DVD rental service evolved into the world's leading entertainment destination in under a decade. Netflix could have simply focused their efforts on delivering a great streaming experience, licensing content from production houses and making it accessible to anyone with access to the internet. But with their success, it wouldn't be long before others followed. They needed to find a solution to maintain customer loyalty, and that solution came through the prioritization of both form and function in their original content.

By moving entertainment into an online streaming platform, Netflix had millions of data points at their disposal. This data showed them which Hollywood stars were trending, what storylines mattered to different viewer demographics, which genres drove the most views, and much more. They used this data to inform the creation of bingeworthy and game-changing original content, combining production value with stories that were sure to inspire viewership.

Key Takeaway Quality visual content perfectly balances form and function. When one is prioritized above the other, the perceived quality of the content will be negatively impacted.

TODAY'S AUDIENCES HAVE TWENTY-FOUR-KARAT-GOLD EXPECTATIONS

Our perceptions of quality have greatly evolved over the years, and today's media landscape has elevated our expectations beyond imagination. Streaming services such as Netflix, Hulu, and Amazon Prime

have drastically altered the world of visual storytelling and entertainment through their focus on original content. Thanks to these services, we all expect blockbuster entertainment at the push of a button, and there's no going back.

By letting user preferences guide storytelling, Netflix and services like it have created a world in which quality entertainment is the daily norm, not the exception. Gone are the days when families wait for the hit Thursday-night lineup of *Seinfeld, Friends,* and *ER.* Today, we make our own lineups every night of the week, combining hit sitcoms and motion pictures of the past with a constant barrage of new releases.

Today's entertainment is star-studded, written to keep us on the edges of our seats for hours on end, and produced for 4K television sets to provide a movie-going experience in our own living rooms. Streaming content delivers twenty-four-karat-gold value to audiences around the world, and all brands must now compete to provide the same level of quality to their customers.

This shifting set of consumer expectations is leading to the death of one of the longest-standing forms of visual storytelling in modern times: television. Assurance, tax, and consulting giant PwC reports that, in 2018, Netflix surpassed consumer broadcast television as a primary source of household entertainment (Figure 3.3). This follows a multi-year trendline in which more and more viewers are moving to the platform to get their content.

Pay-TV vs. Netflix subscribers

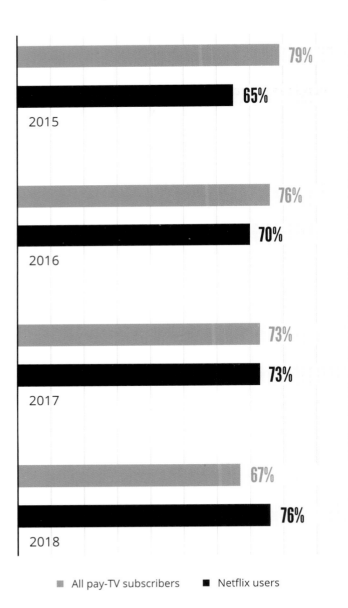

Figure 3.3
Source: PwC, "A New Video World Order."

Revenue Growth Is 50% Slower Than Expenditure Growth

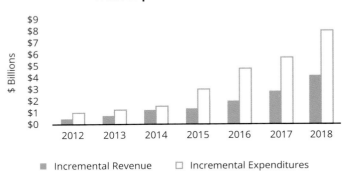

Figure 3.4
Source: Trainer, "Netflix's Original Content Strategy Is Failing."

But, while Netflix's strategy has disrupted the idea of "engaging" content, it has also contributed to an ever more distracted audience. The formula of delivering bingeworthy media has taught consumers to expect nothing but the best at all times, and Netflix is struggling to keep up, as evidenced by a July 2019 stock-price drop reported by David Trainer in Forbes.

As Netflix and services like it continue to throw money at the problem (Figure 3.4), brands have an opportunity to capitalize on the holes left in their audiences' viewing schedules in between seasons. Consumers continue to crave high-quality entertainment, and brands are poised to deliver. In fact, trends show that consumers are beginning to expect equally entertaining content from their favorite brands (Figure 3.5).

**I'd like to watch content created
by brands I like (% agree)**

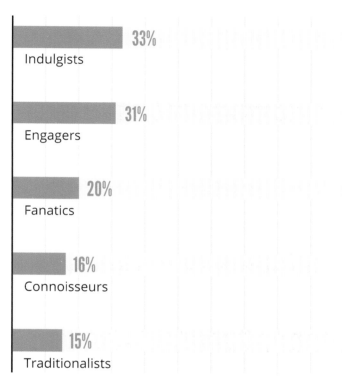

Indulgists — 33%

Engagers — 31%

Fanatics — 20%

Connoisseurs — 16%

Traditionalists — 15%

Figure 3.5
Source: PwC, "A New Video World Order."

Key Takeaway Today's audiences have extremely discerning tastes. Organizations that meet their expectations will gain long-term loyalty. Those that lead with low-quality or cheap-feeling content, however, risk losing the trust and faith of their customers.

With such easy access to amazing content at our disposal, it's no wonder that 94 percent of first impressions are based entirely on design. To succeed in today's content marketplace, brands must deliver high-quality visual content at all times. If they lead with poor form and function, they risk losing brand loyalty and trust in the best-case scenario—and their entire business in the worst.

PART TWO:
8 RULES OF VISUAL COMMUNICATION

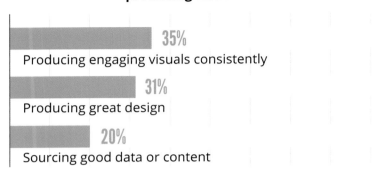

Marketers reported the following challenges when producing visual content:

35%
Producing engaging visuals consistently

31%
Producing great design

20%
Sourcing good data or content

Figure P2.1
Source: Khoja, "14 Visual Content Marketing Statistics to Know for 2019."

While understanding the environmental and instinctual response to modern visual media won't make you a great content producer overnight, it provides an important lens through which to view the world around you. This foundation will help you determine strategies that can break the mold and garner the attention of a diverse array of audiences.

But consistently creating high-quality visual content requires more than theory. In the chapters that follow, I explore eight rules that any good visual communicator must follow to ensure success. Whether you are creating visual content on your own or overseeing a talented designer, the pages that follow will provide you with critical guidelines against which to measure all of your content.

The chapters in part 2 of this book are broken into three sections each. The first section will introduce a specific rule while providing the data-backed context that informs it. The second section will include an exercise to test your understanding of the rule. Some exercises are easy, while others will require that you spend some time at your computer, with a colleague, or with a pen and paper. The final section will summarize key takeaways to apply to your own visual strategy.

Please consume this section of the book in whatever way—and whatever order—is most efficient for you. You may choose to read each chapter opening only, then come back to all of the exercises, and later return to review all of the key takeaways. You may choose to just pick one track to follow, such as doing all of the exercises. Or you may choose to read each chapter in full before moving onto the next.

In the final chapter of part 2, I provide exceptions to some of these rules. While it would be great to deliver content that follows each rule to perfection, sometimes a rule must be broken to ensure the most effective delivery of information. Let these rules act as guideposts, but your ultimate North Star should always be your target audience and the actions you want them to take when viewing your content. Sometimes you will need to break these rules in order to achieve your goals, and that's OK.

By combining the theory delivered in part 1 of this book with the actionable practices defined in the rules that follow, you'll have the necessary tools to produce visual content that engages any audience, improves comprehension, and gets amazing results.

CHAPTER 4

RULE 1: ALWAYS THINK ABOUT CON-TEXT (IT'S A *CON* WHEN THERE'S TOO MUCH TEXT)

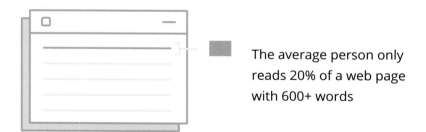

The average person only reads 20% of a web page with 600+ words

Figure 4.1
Source: Nielsen, "How Little Do Users Read?"

When faced with more than six hundred words of copy, the average person only reads 20 percent of the text placed in front of them (Figure 4.1). That's only 120 words, the length of about two tweets. In a world where content can make or break your brand, the ways in which you respond to this fact will determine how successful your content is.

To put this into perspective, consider how you would react to a similar scenario. If you only had fifteen minutes to consume content, would you opt to read a well-written article about your topic of interest or would you prefer to watch a video on the same topic instead (Figure 4.2)? This question was posed to a diverse set of respondents, and 66 percent opted to watch a video rather than read a lengthy article.

With only 15 minutes to consume content, audiences prefer to ...

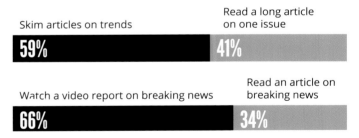

Figure 4.2
Source: Adobe, "The State of Content: Expectations on the Rise."

Today's consumers balk at reading assignments and demand visual content instead—as part 1 of this book has shown. Despite this, brands continue to deliver "visual communication" that combines long-form text with illustrations and iconography in the hopes of satisfying audiences' voracious appetite for visual media. But when the text outweighs the iconography and illustrations, the resulting content is far less engaging and won't garner the same attention as a piece that truly leads with visual communication as its foundation.

For example, how often have you seen an "infographic" executed like the one in Figure 4.3?

This example shows a fairly typical execution of a "quick reference" slide or guide and is in line with what many would consider an "infographic." It is meant to summarize key findings and ensure they are easy to digest. But with this much text and no data visualization, it's really not at all easy to digest— not for audiences who already read just one-fifth of the text on most web pages. As a result, this isn't true visual communication; it is instead a reading assignment with subtle visual cues.

The example breaks one of the most important rules of visual communication. **Always think about context: it's a *con* when there's too much text.**

GENERATION Z & THE POWER OF VIDEO

68

Average number of videos Generation Z watches daily

5+

Number of platforms where Gen Z watches video every day

82%

of all web traffic will be video by 2022

99%

increase in branded video content views on YouTube, 2016–2017

48%

of smartphone users are more likely to make a purchase if a company includes an instructional video on their app or mobile site

Figure 4.3
Source: Adobe, "The State of Content: Expectations on the Rise."

EXERCISE: HOW LONG WILL COMPREHENSION TAKE?

To best exemplify this rule, imagine all of the supporting text shown in Figure 4.3 disappeared and all that remained were the visualizations and headlines. To see what that looks like, view our next "infographic" example in Figure 4.4.

As you look at the design in Figure 4.4, take a moment to ask yourself the questions on the next page as quickly as you can.

CRAS QUIS ODIO ET VELIT

68

Lorem ipsum dolor sit amet, consectetur adipiscing elit

 5+

Pellentesque eu elit vel orci fringilla suscipit

 **82%**

lorem ipsum dolor sit amet

99%

mauris porttitor nisl non felis porttitor laoreet

 **48%**

etiam volutpat turpis sit amet mauris pellentesque, a elementum nisl

Figure 4.4
Source: Adobe, "The State of Content: Expectations on the Rise."

▸ What is the main topic of the piece?

▸ What is at least one key takeaway from the piece?

▸ What do the numbers mean?

Now look back at the version in Figure 4.3. Read through it and time yourself as you do.

▸ How long did it take?

▸ Did you give up reading and jump back into this book?

▸ If so, how long did it take before you gave up?

According to three studies outlined in the journal *Behaviour & Information Technology,* the average person only takes fifty milliseconds to form an opinion of the content they view. This doesn't mean that it takes fifty milliseconds to discern meaning from visual content; it only suggests that this is the time required to judge that content.

But how quickly can our brains truly derive meaning from a single image? Mary Potter, an MIT professor of brain and cognitive sciences, sought to answer this question, as an article in *MIT News* explains. Working with a computer to process images at rapid-fire speeds, Potter and fellow colleagues presented a series of visuals to their test subjects.

It quickly became clear that subjects easily processed images after viewing them for only eighty milliseconds, so the MIT team decided to keep pushing the limits of the test. They tried fifty-three

milliseconds, then forty, then twenty-seven, and finally concluded the study at thirteen milliseconds simply because it was the fastest rate the computer monitor could display images to a viewer.

While subjects did not perform as well when viewing images at thirteen milliseconds when compared to eighty, they were still able to extract a clear meaning from the images they saw. Potter concluded that, in just thirteen milliseconds, "what vision does is find concepts. That's what the brain is doing all day long—trying to understand what we're looking at."

In comparison, our brains take far longer to infer meaning from text. The average adult reads 238 words per minute, according to a 2019 meta-analysis. This breaks down to less than 4 words per second. There are very few sentences that—unaccompanied by visual content—drive significant meaning in four words or fewer, so it's best to assume that it takes at least two seconds for the brain to take in a full sentence. And that doesn't even consider the length of time needed to process and store the information contained within that sentence.

Clearly, leading with too much text can negate the purpose of visual communication, because text is simply less efficient. When the preceding "infographic" is stripped of its text and left with just visuals, it is impossible to make any sense of it. Because the text must be read to understand what the visuals are trying to communicate, we can conclude that it's not true visual communication.

Key Takeaways Consumers crave quality design and proper visual communication, yet brands continue to deliver text-heavy content combined with simple iconography in an attempt to meet the needs of their audiences. Countless designs just like the examples in this chapter are released online every day. If you let visuals tell your story, using text only to complement and elevate that story, you'll easily stand out from the crowd and amaze your audience in the short thirteen-millisecond window of opportunity that's in front of you. So to be sure you're creating great visual content, here are two key steps that will ensure you adhere to this rule:

1. Design your visual content using lorem ipsum text where your copy will go. This will force you to tell your story with visuals rather than words.

2. If you have to spend time reading to identify even a single takeaway from the content, it's not proper visual communication. Rework the design until a few colleagues or friends can at least identify the topic without reading.

CHAPTER 5

RULE 2: SMALL VISUAL CUES HAVE A LARGE IMPACT

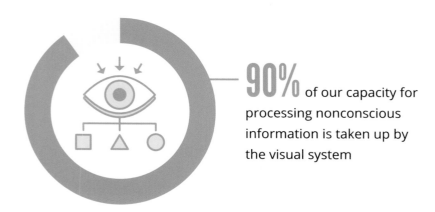

90% of our capacity for processing nonconscious information is taken up by the visual system

Figure 5.1
Sources: Dijksterhuis et al., "The Unconscious Consumer"; Blanchfield, Hardy, and Marcora, "Non-conscious Visual Cues [...]."

In 1957, a market researcher and social physiologist by the name of James Vicary coined the term "subliminal advertising" in the context of his now-infamous popcorn experiment. In that experiment, which was supposedly conducted on 45,699 moviegoers attending a film called *Picnic*, Vicary played 0.03-millisecond flashes of phrases like "Hungry? Eat Popcorn!" or "Drink Coca-Cola" on screen during the film. Vicary declared success, claiming that these subtle cues resulted in an 18.1-percent increase in Coca-Cola sales and a 57.5-percent increase in popcorn sales.

This experiment was later debunked, with one core argument against its findings involving the speed at which the mind can process text in comparison with visuals. Critics argued that the experiment would be more believable if pictures of popcorn and Coca-Cola had been used instead of text. Since the subconscious mind cannot process text-based information nearly as fast as it can visual cues, researchers could not substantiate Vicary's claims.

Regardless of these problems with the popcorn experiment, a widespread interest in the potential of subliminal advertising took hold. Shortly after Vicary published his findings, a report titled "The Operational Potential of Subliminal Perception" outlined the Central Intelligence Agency's own research plans for subliminal messaging. By 1974, the Federal Communications Commission (FCC) had banned the use of subliminal advertising in all television and radio broadcasting, noting that it was "contrary to public interest."

But brands still found a way to prevail. Rather than taking the approach outlined in the popcorn experiment, brands opted to use product placements to deliver subconscious visual cues that would grow loyalty and sales. When Elliot lured ET into his house using a trail of Reese's Pieces, Hershey's saw a 65-percent increase in profits! Director Steven Spielberg's first choice for the movie was to use M&M's, but the candy's manufacturer, Mars, turned him down.

Clearly, **small visual cues have a very large impact.** When it comes to visual communication, the smallest design choices you make can sometimes be more important than the elements that take up the majority of your content.

If we were not so susceptible to small visual cues driving our actions, this practice of product placement would not be experiencing the rapid growth it is today. But thanks to the wide variety of visual entertainment available to us—including video games, digital streaming, television, print, cinema, and more—this market is experiencing its best years ever. Data and analysis leaders PQ Media projected that US product placement revenues would exceed $10 billion in 2018, with brands such as Netflix contributing to the industry's continued success.

TWITTER'S INFAMOUS STAR-VERSUS-HEART WAR OF 2015

Near the end of October 2015, a subtle change to one of Twitter's buttons sent its users into an uproar. The small star button that appeared at the bottom of every post was replaced with a heart. It's important to note that the functionality of the button didn't change, just the icon used for the button itself.

The original purpose of the button was simply to bookmark tweets so that they could be referenced later for any number of reasons. Twitter had chosen not to use a bookmark icon and instead used a star shape when first introducing this functionality. Had a bookmark icon been used, it's possible they could have avoided what happened next.

A star—an image that was up for interpretation depending on the context—meant that user actions could expand beyond simply saving a tweet to reference later. Instead, the button became a tool used to fuel heavy debate within the platform. Users treated the star button as a kind of virtual microphone drop. When they found themselves in an argument with another Twitter user, it became common practice for a user to click on the star button as a signal that they were done with the exchange and had had the last word.

Twitter realized that the subconscious response to the star was the problem. To combat the negativity that sometimes coincided with the star, Twitter chose to change the button's icon, and nothing else.

Twitter had shifted an image that made up less than 1 percent of its site design, but users reacted viscerally. This seemingly small visual shift resulted in a broad outcry among those who felt wholly disrupted by the change (Figure 5.2). That's because heart and a star convey two very different meanings. A star can suggest any variety of meanings, whereas a heart is the near-universal symbol for love. Put into the context of a social network like Twitter, the heart implies condoning a message, liking something, or even liking the messenger.

Suddenly, Twitter users could no longer interact with the bookmark tool in the same way. One simple symbol of love was enough to infuriate an entire user base and completely change how they interacted with the tool. Think about it: if you were in a heated argument, would you end it with a heart icon?

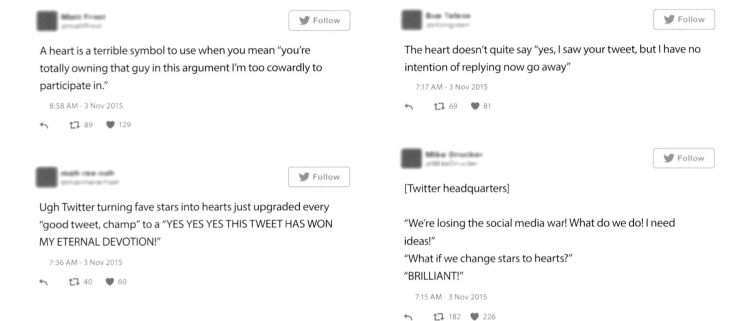

A heart is a terrible symbol to use when you mean "you're totally owning that guy in this argument I'm too cowardly to participate in."

8:58 AM - 3 Nov 2015

89   129

The heart doesn't quite say "yes, I saw your tweet, but I have no intention of replying now go away"

7:17 AM - 3 Nov 2015

69   81

Ugh Twitter turning fave stars into hearts just upgraded every "good tweet, champ" to a "YES YES YES THIS TWEET HAS WON MY ETERNAL DEVOTION!"

7:36 AM - 3 Nov 2015

40   60

[Twitter headquarters]

"We're losing the social media war! What do we do! I need ideas!"
"What if we change stars to hearts?"
"BRILLIANT!"

7:15 AM - 3 Nov 2015

182   226

Figure 5.2

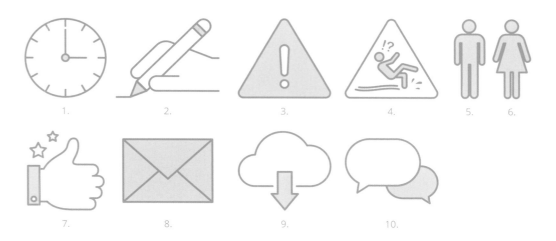

Figure 5.3

EXERCISE: EMBRACING UNIVERSAL IMAGERY

Twitter's star-versus-heart debacle of 2015 offers a great example of how seemingly small visual cues can make a huge impact on the actions of any audience. In the world of visual communication, small visual cues such as universal iconography are important tools for conveying meaning and driving action.

A recycling sign, for example, lets us know how to partition our garbage without a lengthy explanation. Stop lights tell us when to stop, go, or slow down. Visual cues drive many of our actions in daily life, and can share important information.

To put this to the test, look at the icons in Figure 5.3. On a piece of paper, write down one to three words or phrases that you associate with each icon.

When you're done, turn to Figure 5.4 to see if you wrote down words or phrases similar to the icon labels provided. You will likely find that the majority of what you wrote matches the expected conclusions on the following page.

Now take this exercise a step further by visiting TheNounProject.com. By offering "the most diverse collection of icons ever," Noun Project is building a global visual language. Creatives from all over the world submit custom-designed icons to bring meaning to singular words or phrases.

When you visit the site, type a noun or short phrase into the search bar and see the collection of icons that display as a result. You'll quickly find that there are universal symbols for a wide array of words, all of which can be used as inspiration for your own content.

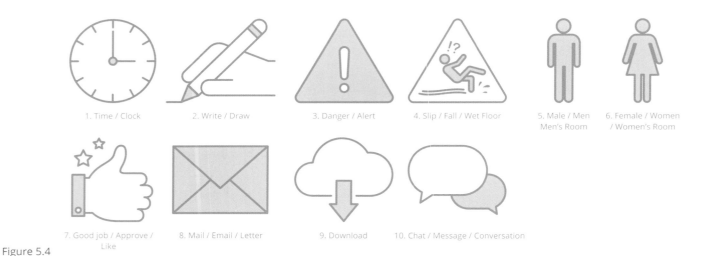

Figure 5.4

Key Takeaways The exercise in this chapter should help you to start focusing on subtle imagery in your daily life. As you go about your day-to-day, keep your eyes peeled for symbols being used to share key information. How do certain icons drive action and others halt you in your steps? How can you use universal iconography to deliver information to your target audience?

Great visual communication leans into the fact that we read similar meaning into popular iconography. Embrace this fact and consider the ways in which small visual cues can best speak to your audience. If you are ever in need of a perfect icon to deliver key information, the Noun Project should be your go-to resource.

CHAPTER 6
RULE 3: THERE'S NO GOLD AT THE END OF THAT RAINBOW

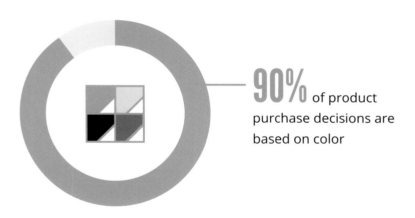

90% of product purchase decisions are based on color

Figure 6.1
Source: Singh, "Impact of Color on Marketing."

A simple search on color theory will yield nearly one billion results on Google. You'll find theorists, marketers, designers, and others sharing their opinions and studies on how color impacts consumer behavior.

Many will argue that shifting a button from green to red will guarantee a boost in conversion rates on your website, or that you consider a different color palette depending on the gender of your target audience. And you can't go down the color-psychology rabbit hole without seeing at least one reference to Robert Plutchick's wheel of emotions (Figure 6.2), which seeks to simplify the correlation between color and feeling with a very specific set of guidelines.

But the concept of color driving emotional responses has been widely criticized by psychologists over the years. While, yes, changing the color of a button on a website may help increase sales, this often happens because the new color choice is bright and stands out in the context of the site's broader design structure. And while a color like red may imply anger or rage, it doesn't seem to inspire a negative reaction when used as the primary brand color for such successful companies as Netflix, Kellogg's, Target, McDonald's, Adobe, and TIME.

CHOOSING THE RIGHT COLORS FOR YOUR VISUAL CONTENT

Your color choices should not be made based on stereotypical associations of colors with emotions. In fact, how color impacts any one individual will greatly depend on their own personal preferences, upbringing, culture, context, and other factors. There simply isn't a one-size-fits-all approach to deriving specific meaning from colors in the way that iconography can send very specific messages to your end audience.

Despite this, the colors you choose and the ways in which you deploy them have the power to engage your audience, further your message, and inspire action. When delivering successful visual content, it's important that you choose your colors wisely. Using too many colors at once will only lead to clutter and cause confusion for your audiences.

Oftentimes, organizations will default to their own brand guidelines to determine the color palette for their content, but this can sometimes be a disservice to the viewer. Studies on marketing theory and the use of color, including an article by Paul A. Bottomley and John R. Doyle in *Marketing Theory,* suggest that brand colors should be used only when the color choice is appropriate to the content or the product being sold. Audiences will judge companies on whether their brand use is appropriate to the information being shared.

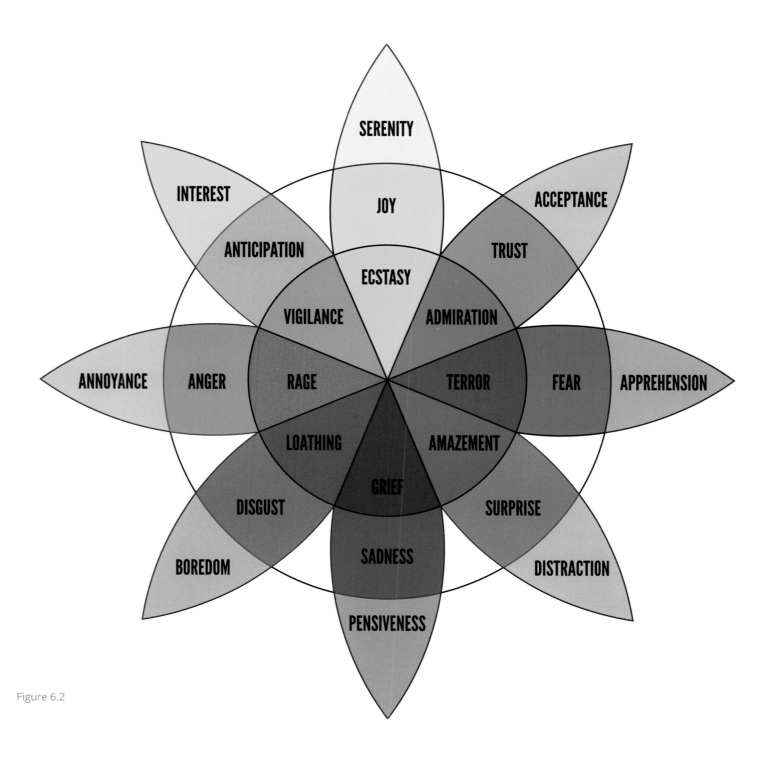

Figure 6.2

So what, then, should marketers and designers do when faced with the need to plan a color palette around their content? Only the most skilled designers can use a rainbow of colors without distracting the viewer (more on this in the final chapter of part 2). For the most part, though, it's best to take a cue from interior designers, who follow the 60-30-10 rule of design.

The concept is simple: choose three principal colors to drive your design. This doesn't mean that you are restricted to only three colors. Instead, if you need to add to your color palette, choose shades of your three main colors to complement the design. One color should act as your dominant hue and should be used 60 percent of the time. Your secondary color should be used 30 percent of the time, while your third color should act as an accent color. Use your third color 10 percent of the time, reserving it for important conclusions, a call-to-action, or to draw the eye to key data points.

If your visual content is lengthy, adhering to the three-color rule is even more important. A viewer will subconsciously recognize when a color is being used for consistency versus to drive meaning or attention. This is especially true in data visualizations, where your secondary color could be used as the main "fill" color for your pie charts and other numbers, while your primary color sets a base that the eye can skim past.

If you use your third color sparingly, it will stand out to your audience as a key indicator of valuable information. In psychology, this concept is called the isolation effect, and it suggests that the brain is more likely to respond to and recall visual cues that stick out as different from the rest. This is often why marketers see an increase in online sales when they treat buttons on their websites with a color that isn't used elsewhere in the design. **This is also why you won't find gold at the end of a rainbow of colors.**

EXERCISE: DO THESE COLORS MATTER?

To better exemplify this rule, on the next page you'll see two designs. With your hand or a piece of paper, cover up the black and white one (Figure 6.4) and only look at the colorful one (Figure 6.3). The text has been purposely replaced with lorem ipsum copy to ensure you are only considering the visual implications of the content.

With the design in front of you, ask yourself the following questions:

1. What is the topic of this piece?

2. What do the colors signify?

3. What did you learn?

4. How does it make you feel?

Now, take a look at Figure 6.4, which shows the same design but with the full text visible and the colors

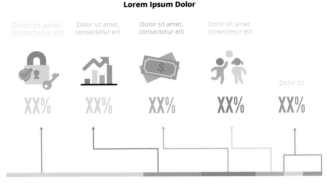

Figure 6.3

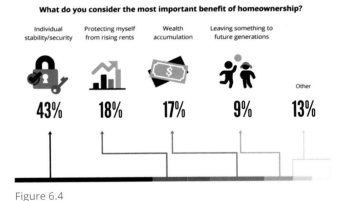

Figure 6.4

shifted to grayscale. You'll likely notice that the colors didn't actually hold any real significance in the full-color version, beyond differentiating the segments in the data visualization. They didn't forward the message in any way but instead created a cluttered aesthetic for the viewer.

We look for meaning in all forms of visual communication, especially when multiple colors are applied to single data visualizations. Rather than

using color intentionally to deliver meaning, Figure 6.3 uses colors only as an aesthetic choice. There isn't a pattern in the usage, so it confuses the viewer rather than making the information easy to digest.

While colors do not inherently inspire emotion, how you apply your color palette should be intentional at all times. Figure 6.5 offers another example to consider. You'll see that the colors chosen are minimal and applied in a way that doesn't feel cluttered or overwhelming. Just like the last example,

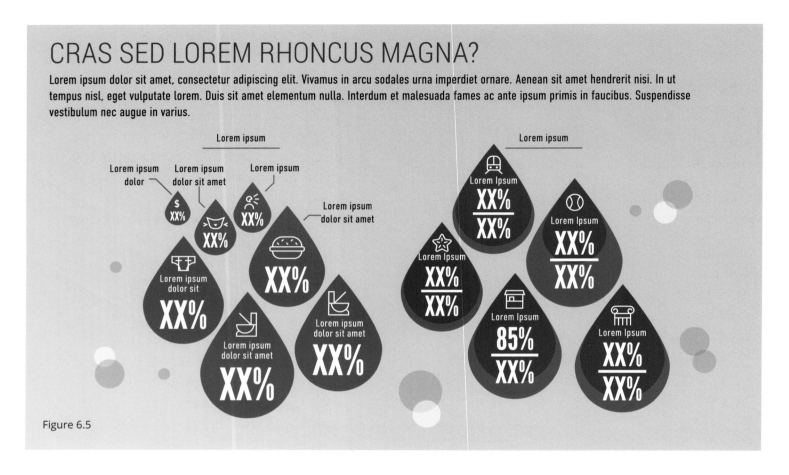

CRAS SED LOREM RHONCUS MAGNA?

Lorem ipsum dolor sit amet, consectetur adipiscing elit. Vivamus in arcu sodales urna imperdiet ornare. Aenean sit amet hendrerit nisi. In ut tempus nisl, eget vulputate lorem. Duis sit amet elementum nulla. Interdum et malesuada fames ac ante ipsum primis in faucibus. Suspendisse vestibulum nec augue in varius.

Figure 6.5

this one purposely has lorem ipsum copy in place of the original content.

For this design, ask yourself the following:

1. What is the topic of this piece?

2. How does it make you feel?

3. What do the colors signify?

4. What did you learn?

Now it's time to see what this infographic is actually about. In Figure 6.6, you'll see the design in full, without any alteration. Review it for up to thirty seconds and then answer the same questions again.

If you're like most people, you likely have different answers after viewing the design within the context of the copy. Before we go on, take a moment to consider the following questions:

1. Prior to reading, what made you think the topic you listed in response to Figure 6.5 was correct?

2. Prior to reading, what made you feel the emotional response that you listed in response to Figure 6.5?

3. Prior to reading, what made you draw conclusions about what you learned in response to Figure 6.5?

It might seem odd that the preceding three questions had to start with "prior to reading," since the bulk of this design leads with visuals over text. Unfortunately, though, the color palette implies a very different meaning than the actual topic. By choosing a clean color palette in combination with a visual depicting water droplets, one would expect that the data shows who *is* washing their hands, versus the very alarming data on how many people are *not* washing their hands.

While specific colors on their own may not actually inspire an emotional response, how those colors are used within the context of illustrations and iconography will drive meaning. By combining a clean color palette with a similarly clean-looking illustration, this piece delivers a far different visual meaning than the information actually being shared.

Key Takeaways While there is widespread debate surrounding the impact of color on a viewer's emotions, color choices do carry forward meaning when placed into the context of visual communication. Our eyes seek out patterns in color to help us make sense of the information we are consuming.

By applying colors strategically—for instance, always using the same color as a "fill" shade in data visualizations—you can help your viewers comprehend the content far more efficiently. Likewise, by choosing colors that align with the topic of your narrative, you can ensure that your audience will embrace that content with ease. And when your color choices don't complement the topic, the best way to avoid clutter and ensure your content is engaging is to keep your palette limited and clean.

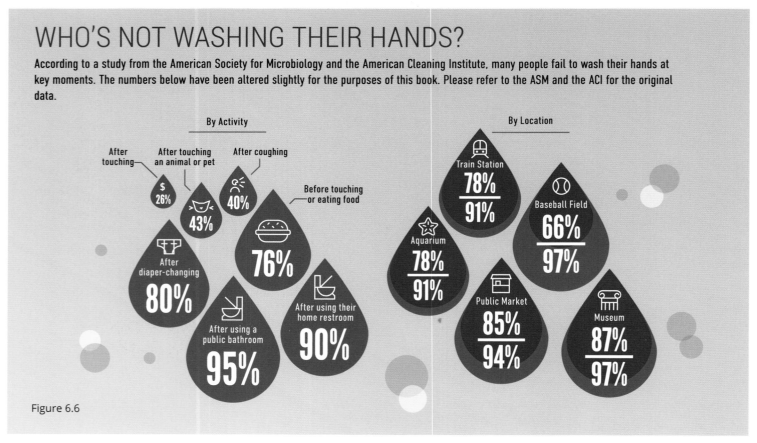

WHO'S NOT WASHING THEIR HANDS?

According to a study from the American Society for Microbiology and the American Cleaning Institute, many people fail to wash their hands at key moments. The numbers below have been altered slightly for the purposes of this book. Please refer to the ASM and the ACI for the original data.

By Activity

After touching — $ 26%

After touching an animal or pet 43%

After coughing 40%

Before touching or eating food 76%

After diaper-changing 80%

After using a public bathroom 95%

After using their home restroom 90%

By Location

Train Station 78% / 91%

Aquarium 78% / 91%

Baseball Field 66% / 97%

Public Market 85% / 94%

Museum 87% / 97%

Figure 6.6

Author Note: The above example was recreated for the purpose of this book. While we altered the colors, we chose to keep the font choices and data visualizations intact. Not only has this design lead with the wrong color palette for the topic, but it also incorrectly represents the data with both overlapping data visualizations and discrepancies in water droplet sizes used to depict percentages. Avoid using the size of like elements to represent a percentage as this method is not an accurate way of visualizing data. In addition to this, the above design breaks the fourth rule of visual communication, which you will learn more about in the next chapter.

CHAPTER 7
RULE 4: GOOD VISUAL STRATEGISTS ASK "WTF?!"

| *"Dogs don't talk in Times New Roman!"*

—Vincent Connare,
Creator of Comic Sans

In 1994, Microsoft was ready to release Windows 95 to the world. As the creator of the first home-computer operating system, Microsoft was faced with the challenge of introducing this new concept to novice computer users. Oftentimes, one of the best ways to explain a complex new product or service is through a visual metaphor, something that Microsoft has always understood. In the case of the first operating system, the company realized that comparing an OS to exploring a house would provide the best user experience, so they came up with Microsoft Bob, pictured in Figure 7.1.

Microsoft Bob featured a customizable home in which users could explore different rooms to access various associated programs. Items in each room were clickable and many were movable to provide easy access for return users. One of the key features of Microsoft Bob was Rover, a virtual dog who acted as a user's tour guide.

When a beta version of Microsoft Bob was released, a typographic engineer at Microsoft by the name of Vincent Connare quickly took notice of Rover's speech bubbles. Why was this dog speaking in Times New Roman? He reeled at the design choice and looked to comics such as *Watchmen* and *Batman,* as well as 1980s advertising, for inspiration. The result was Comic Sans, a font that was inspired by the need to pair visual meaning with the context of the content being delivered.

Figure 7.1 [ ]
Source: Microsoft Bob.

Unfortunately, Vincent's creation was not completed in time for the initial release of Microsoft Bob, but the company saw value in the unique font and packaged it up with a future update to Windows 95 called "Plus!" The font took off, growing in popularity as a unique form of expression for brands and designers alike.

While this font is widely criticized today, many would argue that this is due to oversaturation in the market. The same can be said for fonts like Papyrus—which saw its heyday during the popular release of Avatar—or Lobster, a script font that took the world by storm for a short stint between 2010 and 2014. Regardless of the cause for Comic Sans's demise, it provides a perfect example of how font choices elicit fairly similar emotional responses from audiences of all types.

Even though the suggestion that specific color choices always drive predefined responses is highly debated, the emotional reaction to font choices is considered universal and visceral. This is because fonts are an artistic representation of letters and numbers. They deliver a visual aesthetic long before their individual characters combine to create words. Because of this, all visual strategists must consider font choices as part of their core communication strategy. **If you aren't asking "why this font (wtf)?", you're missing a golden opportunity to connect with your audience.**

Great brand evangelists have followed the WTF rule for decades, carefully considering the font choice for their brand logo before determining complementary fonts to use across all collateral. But marketers and brand-builders alike must be willing to venture outside of their codified brand guidelines to take advantage of font psychology. While brand fonts might work for some web and print design, the font used for a call-to-action in an advertisement can often make a huge difference. So you need to choose that font carefully.

To exemplify this, consider how fonts impact conversion rates online. The experts at Click Laboratory, a well-known firm that focuses on conversion-rate optimization for its clients, often consider how typography impacts user experience and the conversion funnel. When they adjusted font sizes, spacing, and typefaces throughout the Numara Software website, they saw huge success (Figure 7.2).

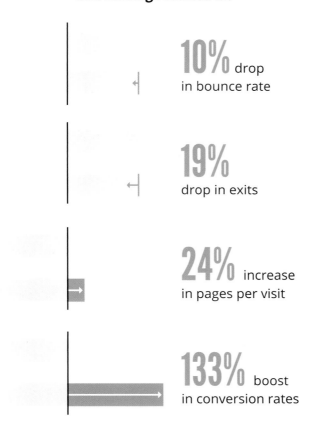

In one case study, increasing font size and leading resulted in:

10% drop in bounce rate

19% drop in exits

24% increase in pages per visit

133% boost in conversion rates

Figure 7.2
Source: Click Laboratory, "Numara Software Case Study."

Font choices don't just drive action, they also inspire trust. In 2012, *New York Times* columnist Errol Morris sought to test this theory with his quiz, "Are You an Optimist or a Pessimist?" The quiz began with an article that covered the topic of enormous asteroids nearly missing earth's surface. Following his own commentary, Morris included a passage from David Deutsch, a visiting professor in the Department of Atomic and Laser Physics at the University of Oxford—in other words, an expert with a pretty impressive résumé. Deustch's quote suggested that humans today are far more prepared than ever to respond to the potential destruction caused by a colossal asteroid hitting the Earth's surface.

Here's the full text of Deutsch's quote:

If a one kilometer asteroid had approached the Earth on a collision course at any time in human history before the early twenty-first century, it would have killed at least a substantial proportion of all humans. In that respect, as in many others, we live in an era of unprecedented safety: the twenty-first century is the first ever moment when we have known how to defend ourselves from such impacts, which occur once every 250,000 years or so.

Following this quote, Morris asked readers two questions with multiple-choice answers:

Do you think Deutsch's claim is true? Is it true that "we live in an era of unprecedented safety"?
Yes: The claim is true
No: The claim is false

How confident are you in your conclusion?
Slightly confident
Moderately confident
Very confident

You might be wondering how this has anything to do with fonts—and the answer is fascinating. Morris, unbeknownst to his readers, had set out to test the perceived efficacy of a statement based entirely on a font choice. To do this, he had Deutsch's statement appear in a different font from the rest of his article. Actually, it appeared at random in six different fonts: Baskerville, Comic Sans, Georgia, Helvetica, Computer Modern, and Trebuchet. It didn't take long before tens of thousands of people had participated in the quiz and Morris had proof that font choices do, in fact, impact a reader's opinion on trustworthiness. See the results in Figure 7.3.

The fonts you choose will deliver a visual message to the viewer before they even read and understand the words. That's why the right fonts will set the tone for your content on multiple levels. They can provide personality, bring further context to the information being shared, and impact the trustworthiness of your brand.

To best put this rule into practice, it's important to first understand the different types of fonts that exist, popular ways of deploying them, and the feelings they elicit. Figure 7.4 provides a complete cheat sheet, spelling out all of these differences in detail.

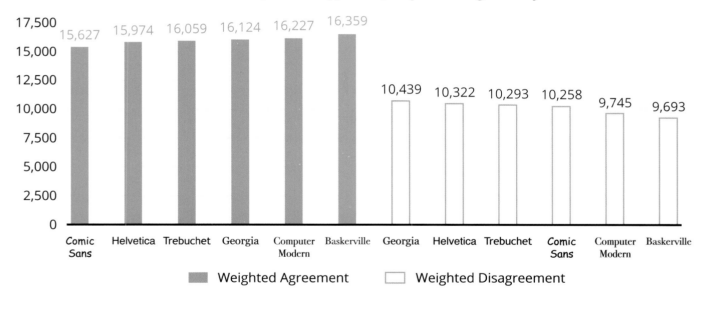

One survey asked if respondents agreed that "we live in an era of unprecedented safety." Based on the font in which the question appeared, respondents gave very different answers:

Figure 7.3
Source: Morris, "Are You an Optimist or a Pessimist?"

Most fonts can be bucketed into the following categories:

Serif Fonts

Characteristics

Considered the most classic of all font types, serif fonts are named after the small lines that are added to the edges of each individual letter. These edges are called "serifs," and they date back to writing styles used in the Roman Empire.

What They Communicate

As a result of their long-time usage, they have earned a position of **trust** and **authority** in most cultures.

When to Use Them

Serif fonts are often used in **print**, because they are considered easier to read in that format.

Size/Weight

As small as eight points in print, standard copy sizes start at twelve points.

Some popular serif fonts include:

Times New Roman

bⅠⅠ·ⅠⅠ·

Georgia

Sans Serif Fonts

Characteristics

A sans serif font is exactly what the name implies: it's a font without the serifs. Sans serif fonts began their ascent in the mid-nineteenth century. At first, they were heavily criticized as crass and unsophisticated. This changed when German designers released some of the most popular sans serif fonts used today, including Helvetica and Futura.

What They Communicate

Considered **clean**, **modern**, and **sophisticated**, sans serif fonts have become more popular than serif in many cases.

When to Use Them

They're generally easier to read **on screen** than a serif font.

Size/Weight

A minimum of sixteen points in size; they look great at very large sizes too.

Some popular sans serif fonts include:

Verdana

Arial

Helvetica

Figure 7.4

Slab Serif Fonts

Characteristics

Similar to their serif cousins, slab serif fonts still have glyphs at the ends of their letters. The difference between slab serif and traditional serif fonts often lies in the glyph itself. Slab serifs overexaggerate their serif lines, making them almost decorative in nature. Slab serif fonts gained popularity among advertisers during the nineteenth century.

What They Communicate

Great slab serif fonts appear best when writing only in uppercase as a form of **yelling a message** to the viewer.

When to Use Them

Often used to **stand out** from the rest of the text on a page, they've been widely utilized on billboards, packaging design, and posters.

Size/Weight

Generally they perform best as a headline or call-to-action.

Some popular slab serif fonts include:

Lexia

Adelle

Clarendon

Script Fonts

Characteristics

Intended to look like handwriting, script fonts can be either formal or casual, depending on the font chosen. A formal script font often resembles the quill-to-parchment calligraphy of the seventeenth and eighteenth centuries whereas casual script fonts can appear like modern handwriting.

What They Communicate

Formal script fonts are often used to signify **prestige**, **history**, and **opulence**. Casual script fonts imply **authenticity** and **approachability**.

When to Use Them

Script fonts should be used sparingly in any piece of visual content, and serve as a tool to **grab attention**.

Size/Weight

They work best in a large font size for legibility.

Some popular script fonts include:

Voltage

Annabelle

Bello

Display Fonts

Characteristics

While the primary font categories of serif, sans serif, slab serif, and script have widely dominated design, new font categories such as display fonts have continued to emerge. Display fonts feel truly designed and overexaggerated in nature. They can be geometric, rounded or bubbled, narrow, tall, short, stubby, etc.

What They Communicate

Display fonts can be **playful** and **quirky** in nature or very **serious** depending on the font family chosen.

When to Use Them

Often used to grab attention in headlines, display fonts **convey very targeted meanings** to their viewers.

Size/Weight

They work best in large-format text, but lose their qualities quickly when sized down to body text.

Some popular slab serif fonts include:

Cooper Black

BUNGEE

Bely Display

Just as the font style can express meaning, the weight and spacing of a font can further that meaning. When considering different font styles, it's important to understand how they appear to a viewer:

Bold	Thin	*Italic*	Condensed
Includes variations like extra bold, medium bold, bold	Includes variations like extra thin, medium thin, thin	Includes variations like bold italic or thin italic	Includes various levels of compression
Loud	Professional	*Elegant*	MODERN
IMPORTANT	Clean	***FAST***	HIP
Authoritative	Sophisticated	*IN MOTION*	Professional
STRONG	Trustworthy	*IMPORTANT*	*Urgent*

WHAT'S IT SAYING?

How font choice helps you convey the right message.

Sans Serif
Neutral
Helvetica Neue, Bold

Serif
Timeless
Times New Roman, Regular

Script, Handwriting
CASUAL
Permanent Marker, Regular

Italic Sans Serif
Let's Go
Aktiv Grotesk, Medium Italic

Italic Serif
"Quote"
Adobe Garamond Pro, Italic

Script
Elegant
Sloop Script, One

Slab Serif
Confirmed
Rockwell, Regular

Black, Extra Bold
BOLD!
Roc Grotesk, Black

Condensed Sans Serif
AUTHORITY
League Gothic, Regular

Modern Serif
Glamour
Didot, Bold

Geometric, Art Deco
RETRO
Mostra Nuova, Bold

Rounded, Soft
Friendly
Sofia Pro Soft, Bold

Monospace
Source Code
Space Mono, Regular

EXERCISE: FONT ASSOCIATION IN ACTION

When people see the font Fraktur, they often find it unsettling but don't know why. It's not a font that is commonly used today, but that's not what makes it unnerving. Fraktur was the font of choice for the Nazi Party and associated propaganda during World War II. When it's used today, it is often used in a similar way, having become an iconic emblem of white supremacy. Fonts elicit meaning, but cultural context equally impacts a viewer's impression of fonts.

When considering font choices for your visual content, you must take into account the context in which your fonts are appearing, both culturally and topically. To best understand this, consider the following:

If you were creating an ad for a cell phone and wanted to showcase the slim design of the phone, which ad shown in Figure 7.5 would appeal most to you?

What if you wanted to showcase a phone's elegance? Which ad in Figure 7.6 would help deliver this concept in the best way?

Figure 7.5

Figure 7.6

As it turns out, a 2013 study authored by Mihyun Kang and Sejung Marina Choi compared the performance of ads very similar to those shown in Figures 7.5 and 7.6. That study found that, depending on the messaging, different fonts performed better in different cases. See Figure 7.7 for the results.

In a 2013 study, ads that emphasized the slimness of the phone performed better with **condensed typefaces:**

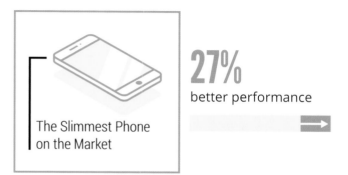

When ads emphasized the elegance of the phone, the opposing font saw better results:

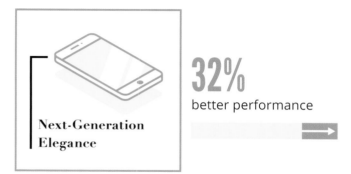

Figure 7.7

Here's another way to consider an exercise like this. In Figure 7.8, you'll see five fonts and five topics. The fonts on the left do not connect with their topics on the right. Can you match these fonts to their appropriate topic?

Match each topic with the appropriate font. The answers are in Figure 7.9.

Figure 7.8

Check out these answers to the exercise in Figure 7.8.

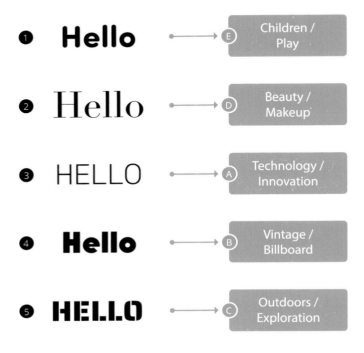

Figure 7.9

You'll notice that some fonts are uppercase, some are lowercase, and some are sentence case. The casing of your font choices also drives meaning and should be considered when you choose a font. You may find that it looks great when presented in one case while it loses its meaning in another.

To best exemplify this, here is the same statement in different fonts:

• WHAT ARE YOU THINKING?

• What are you thinking?

How do these two statements feel tonally different depending on the font?

And between the two options below, which one feels more disarming, and which one feels more demanding?

• DEMANDING

• Disarming

Key Takeaways Entire books have been written on the topic of font psychology (you can find my favorites in part 3 of this book), making this chapter nothing more than the tip of a very large iceberg. But one essential takeaway from our discussion here is that, when you consider the goals of your design, it's imperative that you choose fonts that further these goals by inspiring the appropriate emotional responses in your audience. Don't let your brand fonts force you into a box—instead, find ways to expand beyond them to ensure you are considering both cultural and topical context.

To ensure that your design doesn't get taken over by a diverse array of typefaces, consider choosing three fonts at most and treating them much like your color palette:

1. Choose one font to act as your body copy, taking up the bulk of your design. This font should be thin or medium weight, at least sixteen points in size, and sans serif if you are trying to reach a broad audience.

2. Choose a second font to act as your headline and subhead copy. This font can range between thin or heavy weights, but pick one weight and stick with it for your design. Don't mix weights unless you plan to use the same font for headers as you will for body copy.

3. Finally, choose a font for your main title, any important numbers or call-outs, and your call-to-action. This should be your least-used font, but can be displayed at a large font size. This can also range from thin to heavy in weight, depending on your topic and target audience. But again, pick one weight and stick with it unless you are using the font for body or header copy as well.

For efficiency's sake, try to first choose between serif or sans serif as the main foundation for your fonts. Very skilled designers can mix serif and sans serif fonts in a single design, but it isn't recommended if you are new to design or cannot work with a talented designer.

Finally, if you want to delve deeper into this topic, a list of tools to help you choose your fonts as well as a selection of recommended reading are provided in part 3 of this book.

CHAPTER 8
RULE 5: AVOID THE STIGMA OF STOCK

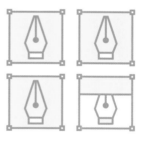

3.3x more marketers

say that original, custom graphics drive the most engagement compared with stock photography

Figure 8.1
Source: Khoja, "14 Visual Content Marketing Statistics to Know for 2019."

Let me introduce to you to the Everywhere Girl (Figure 8.2). In 1996, while Bill Gates was writing his iconic "Content Is King" essay, Jennifer Anderson was graduating college. To make some money and start paying off student debts, she posed for a stock photo shoot. Keep in mind that this was a time when the internet was just starting to take off. Stock-photo sites were in their infancy and rarely could someone simply browse a portfolio and directly download high-resolution photos. Instead, brands were accustomed to stock-photo subscription services that delivered images via CD-ROM.

Brands would pore over the images they received and add them to their marketing collateral, but without an online tool to show the number of downloads an image received, they had no way of knowing what other companies out there were using the same image.

In Jennifer's photo shoot, she was wearing a blue, knit ski cap over her blond hair, a white-shell choker, a leather jacket over a preppy sweater, and a backpack slung over one shoulder. She was tall, pretty, and had an endearing smile. She was the epitome of a late-'90s college student. But she was one of many models in the group of shared photos. No one could have predicted that so many organizations would find Jennifer's photos to be their favorite of the bunch.

By 2004, Jennifer's photos had been used in a wide variety of ad campaigns, making her the face of college girls everywhere. Audiences began to take notice, and online communities appeared overnight

Figure 8.2

with the dedicated goal of reporting sightings of her. She was dubbed the "Everywhere Girl," with one forum on technology news site the *INQUIRER* claiming more than 85,600 sightings.

Her images were so popular that they led to one of the largest marketing blunders of the time. Dell and Gateway, two competing personal computing companies, both used Jennifer's photos in their annual back-to-school campaigns in 2004. It was an embarrassing situation for both brands; it not only confused audiences, but also made each brand the butt of many jokes for the months that followed.

While Jennifer's image showed up on a variety of sites and marketing collateral, she was most notably linked to brands such as H&R Block, Microsoft, Greyhound, Samsung, US Bank, and AAA. Jennifer's story is just one of the many out there in which stock imagery hurt a brand's reputation rather than helped it.

THE GROWING AVERSION TO STOCK IMAGERY

For many audiences today, the overuse of stock imagery has transformed it from an engaging form of visual content to an eyesore that must be avoided at all costs. This change has been driven largely by younger audiences, who have encountered a huge variety of stock imagery as its usage has grown in tandem with the rise of the internet. What's more, younger audiences learn about brands through a variety of channels, with social media leading the charge. Stock images lose their appeal in these venues, yet many brands continue to lean on them as the foundation of their visual marketing efforts.

This isn't a new trend. As I write this, the stigma of stock has been growing for more than a decade. Eye-tracking studies from as early as 2010 have helped to prove this distaste for stock imagery in favor of candid, authentic photography. Jakob Nielsen, cofounder of research firm the Nielsen Norman Group, led a 2010 study that measured the eye movements of viewers when they were presented with various types of imagery. He determined that original and real-feeling imagery consistently outperformed posed stock photography. In fact, stock photos largely went ignored by viewers, even when they took up the most real estate on a page.

The problems with stock imagery first lie in the issues this type of content is trying to solve for. The intended goal of stock photos is to provide equal access to ample imagery for organizations of all sizes. Because of this, many stock photos have to establish broad appeal, which can make them vague and unnatural in their execution.

Because stock sites are available to anyone, organizations that rely on them do so at the risk of their brand's originality. As in the case of the Gateway and Dell mishap, brands can't control whether a competitor uses the same imagery. Some competitors may take advantage of this to confuse audiences over which company is the most legitimate. In other situations, that imagery might be tied to a negative ad campaign that could inadvertently hurt the image of other brands using the same photos in different contexts.

With the considerable growth of sites such as Instagram and Snapchat, today's audiences view photography quite differently than ever before. Photography is a way of sharing experiences, and with the continued improvements in smartphone cameras, everyone has the tools at their disposal to *feel* like professional photographers. This has created a new generation of critical viewers who can instantly recognize when something feels stereotypical or basic rather than candid and approachable.

When businesses opt for original photography over stock imagery both on-site and in their marketing campaigns, they quickly see an impact to their bottom line. Tomer Dean, the tech entrepreneur who cofounded and runs Bllush, helps e-commerce clients grow their business by trading their stock imagery for user-generated content (UGC), such as photographs found on Instagram and similar networks. When testing ads for Nike and Zara, the Bllush team was able to achieve a 300-percent increase in click-through rates by opting for UGC photos over traditional product imagery.

IT'S NOT JUST STOCK PHOTOGRAPHY: STOCK ILLUSTRATIONS POSE RISKS TOO

Of course, stock imagery doesn't just center around photorealistic graphics. Today, stock vector assets are beginning to lose their luster as well. With the growing demand for visual content, marketers are struggling to keep up. As a result, they are often turning to the internet to buy up illustration packs. This poses a few key problems, though:

▸ Just like stock photography, stock illustrations can be used by anyone. This means that brands cannot stand out from the pack. What's more, since these brands lack creative control over the images they utilize, they risk seeing the same illustrations used by a variety of organizations and industries.

▸ Often, a single illustration pack doesn't have all of the elements needed to finalize a long-form piece of content. This either means that

marketers have to rely more on text to drive their message, or that they have to find a different illustration pack to supplement their design.

▸ Illustration packs and icon packs are often sold separately. This makes it very hard to find a set that not only contains every icon you need, but also matches the exact aesthetic style of the illustration pack. This leads to a final design with competing styles.

▸ When a content creator cannot develop custom illustrations that best represent the information, they often end up breaking rule 1: always think about con-text. That's because, to bring meaning to their stock image, they often have to include supporting text. Entirely custom illustration, on the other hand, can always be created to best represent the information with minimal or no text.

To exemplify this, remember the first infographic I ever designed? Take a moment to flip back to Figure AA.1 in "The Accidental Agency" to look at it again.

EXERCISE: WHEN STOCK IMAGERY IS ALL YOU CAN USE

Despite these issues, there is still a time and a place for stock imagery—when it is handled right. In fact, it's quite possible to overcome all of these issues while still taking advantage of the many benefits stock imagery provides, such as its efficiency and affordability.

To succeed with stock imagery, the trick is to find images that have inherently good traits which, once you've purchased the images, can then be elevated through design tools. Let me show you how:

Step 1: Find a stock photo that doesn't feel posed

In general, try to avoid photos in which the hero or a group is looking directly at the camera. As simple as this sounds, it can feel very subjective once put into practice. Some photos with unique camera angles can work, but often eye-level photos feel staged to the viewer.

You'll also want to avoid photos where any people look like they're sitting or standing in unnatural positions, or where their facial expressions feel exaggerated. Consider photos that use unique camera angles when possible, as the unique camera position often caters to a more candid look and feel.

Quick tip: Many stock-image sites are beginning to provide photos that already have filter effects such as high saturation, vignettes, or sepia tones. Those will likely stand out as more candid, but if you need to produce a piece of content with a lot of photography, I suggest avoiding options that already incorporate filters. This is because a single piece of visual content should ensure the photos you use look as if they are part of the same family. If one has filters and others don't, the diverse aesthetics will disrupt the eye.

Step 2: Check the popularity of your photo before purchasing

To avoid the possibility that a stock photo or illustration is already being used by a competitor, consider how popular it is before purchasing it. On some stock sites, you can easily check how many purchases or downloads a photo has. The more popular stock sites, such as iStock and Shutterstock, make this harder to determine.

When faced with a site that won't share this data with the general public, use their search filter tools to improve the likelihood that you'll find a lesser-used image. Often, these sites have a "most popular" filter. By viewing images in that bucket, you'll automatically know that they're more widely used than others.

Some providers also let you filter by publish date. This can often allow you to be one of the first to purchase an image. What's more, you'll find that more recent stock photos are taking heed of today's trends, making it easier to find more forward-thinking photography.

Don't just rely on the stock site data, though. Once you've found a photo you like, it will be important to do a reverse image search to see how many times the image already appears online. With Google, this is very easy. Simply go to images.google.com. Next, drag the image into the search bar. In an instant, Google will provide results showing just how often that particular image appears online.

Step 3: Customize your photo

Simply finding a rarely used, candid photo isn't enough. If you've found it, it's likely others in your

Stock

Custom Stock

Isolate or blur
foreground or
background
elements

Overlay illustrative
elements

Add photo
filters

LOREM IPSUM

DOLOR SIT

Use shape to
frame or
reveal the
photo

Figure 8.3 [ ]

industry have too. To fully overcome the stigma of stock, you need to make your stock image unique to your brand.

Here are the four primary ways to customize your stock:

▸ Add illustrative elements on top of the photo.

▸ Use shapes to frame or reveal the photo in unique ways.

▸ Add photo filters similar to what can be found on a modern smartphone or Instagram.

▸ Use a tool such as Photoshop to isolate or blur foreground or background elements.

Figure 8.3 shows a stock photo that was found using steps one and two above. This photo was then customized using each of the four methods so you can see them in action.

Key Takeaways Today's audiences crave custom visual content above all else. Brands that lead with custom visuals see higher engagement and aesthetic cohesion, and can more easily communicate visually rather than textually. Stock imagery, on the other hand, deters from a brand's unique mark and authentic message. This doesn't mean that stock imagery should be avoided entirely; instead, it should be elevated to meet the bespoke expectations of modern consumers.

There is a time and a place for stock imagery. When it comes to communicating the right message to the right audience, you need to select an appropriate image, then include custom elements with specific goals and parameters in mind.

CHAPTER 9
RULE 6: STAND OUT AT THE COCKTAIL PARTY

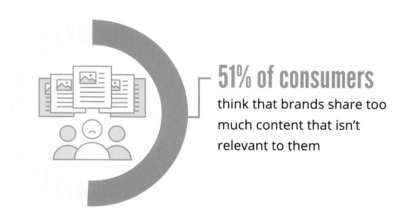

51% of consumers think that brands share too much content that isn't relevant to them

Figure 9.1
Source: Marketo, "The State of Engagement."

In his bestselling book, *How to Win Friends and Influence People,* author Dale Carnegie writes, "Remember that a person's name is, to that person, the sweetest and most important sound in any language."

This notion was proven true in a 2006 study called "Brain Activation When Hearing One's Own and Others' Names," for which psychologists Dennis P. Carmody and Michael Lewis used functional magnetic resonance imaging to study the brain-activation patterns of respondents when hearing a list of names. Within the list was always the respondent's own name. The results concluded that our brains light up more aggressively when hearing our own name in comparison to those of others.

This concept is also considered **"the cocktail party effect."** Imagine you are at a loud, crowded cocktail party with a healthy mix of friends and complete strangers. Conversations are happening all around you, and you're in the middle of an engaging one yourself. Suddenly, you overhear your name come up in conversation in another room entirely. Immediately, your ears perk up and your attention suddenly shifts from your friend's story about their overwhelming workweek to whatever must be going on in that room.

Our brains consistently process information all around us, even if we are not consciously giving the entire surrounding environment our full attention, explains Dr. Rachna Jain in an article for *Social Media Examiner.* This process happens through the reticular activating system (RAS), which helps to determine what we pay attention to and when. In the simplest of terms, the RAS selectively drives our attention to ideas and information that matter most to us, while letting all other information fade away like background noise at a party.

YOUR AUDIENCE WANTS CUSTOM, PERSONALIZED CONTENT

In today's world of information overload, we live in a never-ending cocktail party—one that seems to be getting louder and louder. As a result, brands continue to experiment with personalized content experiences to gain and maintain the attention of their audiences. This comes in many forms: just take a look at Spotify's "Discover Weekly" playlist, which recommends music to listeners based on past preferences; or streaming-media providers that advertise new shows and movies to viewers based on what they watched previously; or sites such as Amazon that tell shoppers what products other, like-minded shoppers also considered. The list goes on.

As brands compete for their audiences' attention, it's the content that feels customized and catered precisely to individual consumers that breaks through the noise. This fact holds true in the world of visual strategy as well. Visual communication is not just about speaking with a universal visual language; if

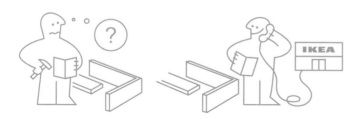

Figure 9.2
Source: IKEA.

you have a target audience to reach, you must speak their visual language.

When considering the visual language of your target audience, you must also consider their cultural context. For example, have you ever looked at the instructions for putting an IKEA product together? While most would agree that IKEA's directions are not as straightforward as we would hope, their designs go a long way toward inclusive customer representation.

That's because IKEA uses an amorphous character known as the IKEA Man (shown in Figure 9.2) to depict any customer going about construction.

Imagine if this character wore a cowboy hat and boots. Would customers in IKEA's home country of Sweden recognize themselves in him? What if the character were more realistically proportioned and wearing a suit and tie? Would a mother-to-be trying to build her new crib see herself in the illustration? Because IKEA has to relate to everyone equally, they chose a character illustration that doesn't discriminate. Not only is the illustration purposely

simple, but the character is disproportionate, thus furthering the notion that he represents a universal symbol rather than a specific demographic.

When speaking to a broad audience, utilizing vague imagery is sometimes important. But it's not too different than trying to make a big announcement at a cocktail party. Some people will listen, while others will be a few drinks in and won't be as eager to give you their attention. Instead, you'll find far more success making visual and narrative choices that speak directly to your target audience.

When developing visual content with a target audience in mind, follow these directives:

▸ **Build your content around a narrative that appeals to your target audience.** For example, are you trying to connect with recent college grads? Appeal to their sense of excitement surrounding the opportunities that lie ahead. Speak to the common problems they may face while entering the workforce or paying off student loans.

▸ **Choose fonts, colors, and an illustration style that best represent the information and appeal to your target audience.** Let's say you're trying to connect with expectant parents. Consider softer blues and pinks, which are often associated with babies. Try a script font for headlines, as these are often used in birth announcements. And choose an illustration style that is playful rather than one that is sleek or technical.

▸ **Use imagery that speaks to the topic and your target audience equally.** For example, what if you're trying to advertise a new, high-performing motor oil? Consider using racing imagery like a checkered flag or banner, a raceway, or sports cars.

▸ **Follow the rule of subtle visual cues.** Imagine you're looking to connect with *Harry Potter* fans. While you can include familiar imagery such as a wand or a Gryffindor scarf, you should also include visuals that only true fans would recognize—for instance, by writing the words "I open at the close" on an illustration of the Golden Snitch.

▸ **Meet your audience on their preferred channel.** Don't just create visual content for your website and hope that your audience will find it. Instead, identify the most trafficked channels where your audience is already engaging. Design content that is sized for ease of viewing on those channels first and foremost. If your narrative is too long for a short-form channel like Twitter, that's perfectly fine. Develop some teaser content that includes a call-to-action to drive your audience to the long-form iteration.

▸ **Design with cultural context in mind.** If you are trying to appeal to a certain demographic, make sure you positively represent them throughout your design. For example, while an ad for a vacuum featuring an overly enthusiastic housewife might have worked in the 1950s, a brand might lose their shirt over similar advertising today.

Visual information has the power to make a very strong impact on its audience. But if that audience isn't considered in the design from the beginning, the visual content you produce may end up being a waste of resources, and could just as easily alienate your audience altogether.

EXERCISE: WHICH APPLE APPEALS MOST TO YOU?

On the next page you'll see two infographics showing roughly the same information yet visualized in two very different ways. One design, entitled "The Insanely Great History of Apple" and shown in Figure 9.3, was initially created by Pop Chart (then called Pop Chart Lab) in 2011. Pop Chart has since updated the design multiple times to incorporate new additions to the Apple family of products. The second design (Figure 9.4), which depicts thirty-five years of Apple product history under the title "The Apple Tree," was created by *Mashable,* also in 2011. For the sake of this exercise, Pop Chart's 2011 version of the design is being used since it's the closest apples-to-apples (pun intended) narrative for comparison.

Take a moment to look at the first infographic, then the second. After you've reviewed them both, ask yourself the following:

1. Which one is your favorite?

2. What makes it your favorite?

3. What don't you like about the other one?

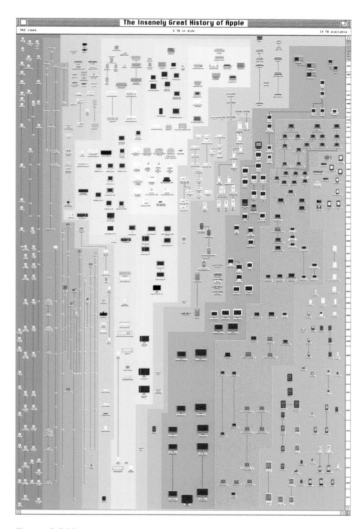

Figure 9.3 [ ]
Source: Pop Chart.

Figure 9.4 [ ]
Source: Mashable.

Since the launch of these designs in 2011, I have been pitting them against each other in a battle over popularity. In every class I teach and at nearly every conference where I've presented, I've asked the audience to tell me which design appeals most to them. Before reading on, take a moment to show both designs to your colleagues, family, or friends. Ask them the same questions that you've answered, and tally the responses.

In my experience, the vast majority (roughly 80 percent) of audiences prefer *Mashable*'s depiction of this information over Pop Chart's. Of course, since this question is always asked in groups, I'm willing to bet that more than 20 percent of respondents would select Pop Chart's design—they just might not want to admit they're in the minority in front of a crowd. For the sake of argument, let's assume the margin of error is 10 percent. That would still be a 70–30 split, making the Mashable design the clear winner.

Why, then, is Pop Chart's design so popular that it has been updated regularly and still sometimes shows as a bestseller on their storefront? The answer is simple: Pop Chart isn't catering to the Everyman—they're catering to a very specific type of Apple fan.

When Pop Chart created "The Insanely Great History of Apple," it did so with the intention of selling a poster online. Mashable, meanwhile, was focused on social engagement and shareability only.

To appeal to its diverse reader base, *Mashable* had to cast a very wide net with its design. The execution is colorful, but the colors don't carry forward any meaning. In fact, product categories aren't even broken down by color. This is a flaw in the execution, because even online critiques of the piece show that viewers spent quite some time trying to determine what the different colors meant.

In *Mashable*'s piece, the illustrations are tame and simplistic. The font choice is playful and trendy for the time, almost as if it were intended as a nod to Twitter's font. When looking to attract social shares, choosing a font that felt like iconic social brands of the time likely helped drive success.

Both designs break the rule of rainbows, but this is a time when that rule can be broken. Good designers can properly execute a very colorful design, and, in this case, using these colors was a clear decision to carry the Apple brand forward. But it appears that this is where the intentional design choices stopped for *Mashable*'s infographic—and where they were just beginning for Pop Chart.

You see, the team at Pop Chart designed with their target audience in mind. They weren't trying to grow readership or social engagement with their design in the way *Mashable* was. They didn't need to cast a wide net. Instead, they understood that getting someone to hit "like" on an image is easy. Getting someone to purchase and frame that image, on the other hand, requires delivering value beyond the quick dose of endorphins one might get from looking at a pretty image.

To deliver a product worth buying, Pop Chart had to consider exactly who the information would appeal to in the first place. More importantly, they had to consider who would want an artful representation of that information hanging in their living rooms. The answer was simple: Apple fanatics.

Apple fanatics are a special breed of tech fan. They know the whole history of Apple, refer to Steve Jobs simply as "Jobs," and are always the first in line to buy the latest release of the iThis or iThat. They are experts, and experts can spot fluff from a mile away. Luckily, the team at Pop Chart considered every detail, creating an image that was filled with visual cues only an Apple fan would truly appreciate.

Consider the following details that Pop Chart prioritized:

▸ **Layout:** The entire design is framed by a Mac OS 8 Finder window motif. Anyone who uses an Apple desktop or laptop views this window multiple times in a given work session. Meanwhile, to bring attention to the historical aspect of the piece, a timeline of dates appears where a scroll bar normally would.

▸ **Product key:** Apple users naturally look for file names within a document window. In the location their eyes would naturally travel (along the top) lives a key that corresponds to the colors in the infographic title and reveals what each colored column represents.

▸ **Colors:** The colors hearken back to the original Apple logo.

▸ **Illustration style:** In the same way that Apple products rely on a clean, minimalist design, the chosen illustration style is minimalist and clean as well. This allows for important details to shine through and showcases the difference between closely linked models. In addition to this, the team at Pop Chart went out of their way to ensure every product was drawn to scale. Pop Chart's cofounder Patrick Mulligan explained this design choice in a *Fast Company* feature: "We needed to figure out exactly how large these machines were, so they could be depicted in the correct relation to one another. We scoured the web to find the dimensions of all these machines, compiling them into an Excel document and applying a 1:20 scale."

▸ **Easter eggs:** Apple has a rich history of incorporating "Easter eggs" (tiny details or experiences hidden within a design, software, and more) into its product design. The team at Pop Chart knew this and included their own in the infographic. The most notable in this version are the number of used and available bytes, which correspond to the birth and death dates of Jobs himself.

While the varying shapes of each column were a decision driven largely by the information being shown, it had an unintended result as well. Many have read into the design choice, assuming that it was a premeditated visual metaphor referencing the legendary moment that Steve Jobs first dreamt up Apple. As the story goes, Jobs was running through a field on an acid trip when the idea for Apple first came to him.

Knowing all of this, has your opinion of which design is the best changed or remained the same?

Key Takeaways If you were part of the majority that felt Mashable's design far outweighed Pop Chart's, it's likely your perspective has changed now that you've had a moment to learn about the design thinking involved. While Pop Chart's design might not appeal to the Everyman, it does appeal to the company's target audience. And while the design might not visually communicate to you specifically, there are more than enough subtle visual cues to hook the intended audience in milliseconds. In other words, this audience was lost in a cocktail party and Pop Chart's design called their name.

Had the team at Pop Chart chosen to design for the everyday consumer instead of a more targeted audience, the infographic wouldn't have exhibited the same amount of popularity or staying power as it has. Instead, they used the topic to determine their audience and then let that audience guide the design. Here are ways you can do the same:

1. If you don't have a lot of information on your audience, take some time to research who they are, what they like, and what interests them. This will help you build a profile and make decisions based on that profile.

2. If your audience is an expert on the topic, don't dumb the information down or add any unnecessary fluff. This will only offend them, because it gives the impression that your brand doesn't even know who they are.

3. Even if you *are* trying to sell to everyone, center your campaigns around predefined audience types. This will allow you to target your content specifically to each customer persona, a strategy that will likely see greater success than you'd find by casting a wider net.

When a group is asked to choose between an intricate design that they might spend hours viewing versus a design that's primarily just eye candy, they might choose to turn their attention to the safer design. But just like at a busy cocktail party, you're rarely in a position to speak to everyone equally. Show up to the party with predefined goals and speak only to the audiences that will help you achieve those goals.

CHAPTER 10
RULE 7: USE PROPER DATA VIZ THROUGHOUT

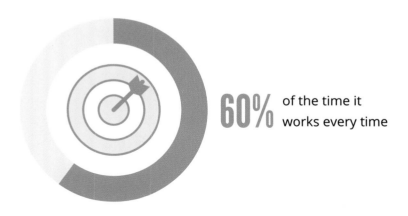

Figure 10.1
—Brian Fantana
"Anchorman: The Legend of Ron Burgundy"

Whether in school or in the workplace, the majority of us have had to either read or create charts and graphs at some point in our lives. This graphic representation of data, called "data visualization" or "data viz," has been our go-to method for understanding how numbers correlate to one another for centuries. In fact, the first-ever line and bar graphs were developed as early as 1786, when William Playfair released The Commercial and Political Atlas.

Playfair wanted to compare the total amount of exports to the total amount of imports in Scotland over a single-year period (from 1780 to 1781), broken down by source/destination. To chart total numbers,

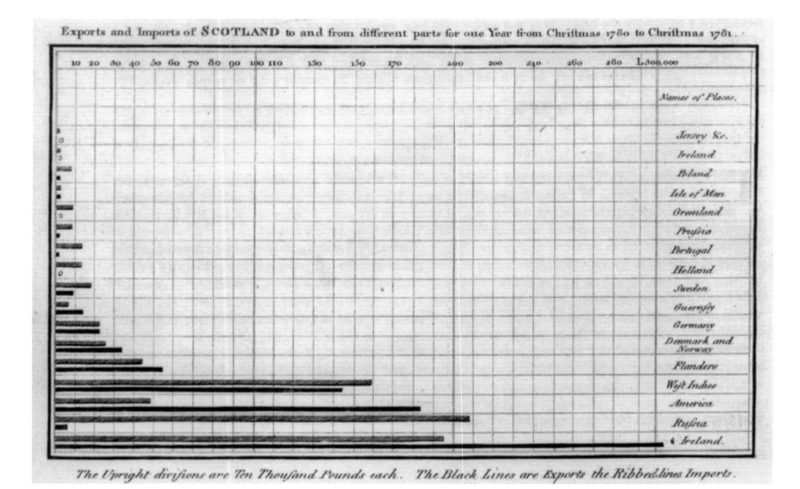

Figure 10.2 [ ]

identify locations, and differentiate imports from exports, he realized that a combination of bars and scales would do the trick. The result was the first recorded bar graph in history, pictured in Figure 10.2.

At the time, Playfair was navigating uncharted waters, but today, charts and graphs are extremely commonplace. Over the years, tools such as Excel, Tableau, and PowerPoint have made it extremely easy for us to quickly visualize data sets and share them widely.

Given this, you might be surprised to learn that mistakes in data visualizations run rampant in the world of visual content. For instance, it's common to assume that comparing numbers to one another always requires a bar chart, while showing percentages always requires a pie chart. Or sometimes it's assumed that a bar chart can have multiple scales, or worse, no scale at all.

We have taken charts and graphs for granted. Because they're so easy to produce, we automatically assume they're accurate. But tools such as Excel and PowerPoint just visualize the numbers we input; they don't consider the context of those numbers to determine their best graphical representation.

To identify the right visualization to use, we must first consider the story we are trying to tell, just as Playfair did. We must consider how the associated numbers correlate to one another and to the context in which the data was collected. Without this information, the potential that the data will be improperly visualized

grows exponentially—an issue that can greatly hinder the success of any visual content strategy and the reputation of the brand that publishes that incorrect data viz.

CASE IN POINT: DON'T SKIP THE SCALE

During the heated debate over the Affordable Care Act (ACA) in 2014, a Fox News broadcast displayed a data visualization suggesting that the demand for health care under the ACA was lower than expected, with the implication that the ACA was not successful. Figure 10.3 shows a screenshot from that broadcast.

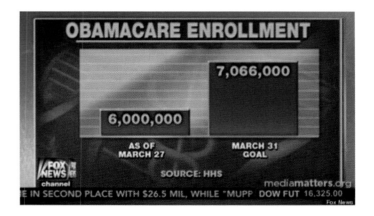

Figure 10.3

After an initial glance at this image, we might quickly agree with the assertions noted in the broadcast. But upon closer inspection, we can see that the scales are completely off. By starting the x-axis at approximately

5,250,000 and not labeling it as such, the March 27 data appears to total just 30 percent of the 7,066,000 goal. This disparity signals to a viewer that there is a very long way to go to reach the end goal, with only days left.

But in reality, 6,000,000 is 85 percent of the end goal. That's a significant difference. In fact, there was plenty of time left to achieve the Obama administration's goal of more than seven million enrollees.

For comparison, check out Figure 10.4 to see how this data should have been visualized.

Obamacare Enrollment

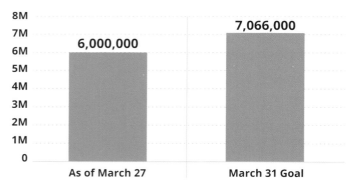

Figure 10.4
Source: United States Department of Health and Human Services.

When visualizing data, it's very important to give viewers all relevant context to they can draw their own conclusions from unbiased visualizations. Manipulating scales, start points, and layout can lead to incorrect data interpretation. At best, this is an unintentional misrepresentation of information; at worst, it can deliberately mislead the audience in order to further a particular agenda.

ADHERE TO THE COMMON LANGUAGE OF DATA VIZ

When it comes to data visualization, we share a common visual language that ensures fluency in communication and understanding. Pie charts always add up to 100 percent. Horizontal timelines show past on the left and the future to the right. The list goes on.

Designing contrary to this visual vernacular will only cause confusion. As an example, check out the line graph in Figure 10.5, which was released by Reuters in 2014 and quickly incited political debate.

Number of murders committed using firearms

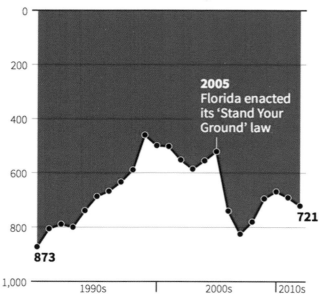

Figure 10.5
Source: Florida Department of Law Enforcement.

Remember the phrase we all learned in school to best differentiate the y-axis from the x-axis? "Y to the sky!" Inherent in the phrase is the assumption that the bottom of the y-axis symbolizes the lowest number in the data set, while the highest number in the set lives at the top of that axis. In other words, up means up and down means down. If you were to strip away all the labels from any line or bar graph, you would still be able to identify trends because of this standard expectation.

The Reuters graphic, however, inverted this rule by flipping the y-axis. Instead of seeing the passage of the "Stand Your Ground" legislation as a potential catalyst for the marked increase in gun deaths in the early 2000s, the viewer is led to mistakenly conclude that this law coincided with an immediate decrease in gun deaths.

Figure 10.6 shows how this graph should have been visualized instead.

Gun deaths in Florida

Number of murders committed using firearms

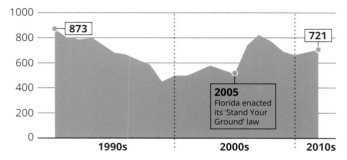

Figure 10.6
Source: Florida Department of Law Enforcement.

With the Reuters example, it's not clear if the graph choice was made because they wanted to add a unique spin on their data visualizations or because of an attempt to lead the viewer to incorrect conclusions. That uncertainty hurts the Reuters brand and provides a perfect example of why properly visualizing data is imperative to any visual strategy.

DRESSED-UP DATA VIZ CAN DO MORE HARM THAN GOOD

But what if it's clear that your intent was not to mislead viewers? Are mistaken representations of data forgivable? One of the biggest temptations many face when first setting out to visualize data is trying to dress up the visualization so that it doesn't feel "boring." There is often a fear that traditional charts or graphs won't engage a viewer. In reality, there are many ways to improve the aesthetics of a pie chart or bar graph without it feeling boring at all. The line chart in Figure 10.6, for example, shows this through its clean, stylized look and attention-grabbing call-out boxes.

While it's a good practice to ensure your charts and graphs don't look like products of Excel, avoiding a traditional bar graph or pie chart is often a lost opportunity. Data visualization has been around for centuries. Charts and graphs speak a universal language, and dressing them up unnecessarily just prevents us from creating true visual communication.

As an example, take a look at Figure 10.7, which shows an area graph from the NBC Nightly News.

Figure 10.7

The designer clearly aimed to make this data more hard-hitting with the integration of a US map. But a map is, in itself, a visualization of information and data. Combining the map with the area graph changes the entire meaning of the graph. Here is a breakdown of the problems this choice causes:

▸ It's just plain difficult to read. Too many visuals are packed together, confusing the viewer.

▸ Whenever you layer red and blue over a map of the United States, your viewers will immediately think the image is about politics.

▸ The West Coast appears stuck in 1960, while the East Coast has time-traveled to 2060.

▸ Asian Americans only appear to live in Maine and Washington State; African Americans live exclusively across a thin band in the North, and so forth.

▸ The scale is incorrect. By not sticking to a standard graph shape, percentages do not match up with the amount of space filled.

There are quite a few different approaches the designer could have taken to avoid these issues. Figure 10.8 shows just one possible execution.

Changing Face of America

Percent of total US population by race and ethnicity, 1960–2060

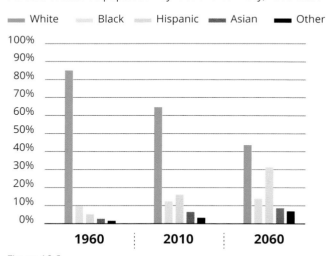

Figure 10.8

Issues like these have occurred throughout the news cycle for generations, but they have skyrocketed since consumer demand for visual content has brought new value to data visualizations. In his book, *How*

Charts Lie: Getting Smarter about Visual Information, author and data visualization expert Alberto Cairo draws attention to this trend by presenting myriad charts and graphs that were either misunderstood by the designer or wholly misrepresented by the publisher.

Cairo addresses multiple types of data visualization mistakes that publishers should avoid, but also warns audiences of the need to improve their own literacy, or graphicacy, on the topic. Graphicacy, he notes, "is the ability to interpret visuals." He warns that today's audiences find charts and graphs persuasive because they expect data visualizations to be objective. Unfortunately, he continues, "charts may lie in multiple ways: by displaying the wrong data, by including an inappropriate amount of data, by being badly designed—or, even if they are professionally done, they end up lying to us because we read too much into them or see in them what we want to believe."

As data visualization mistakes persist, the brands that publish and share them become less reliable and audiences begin to lower their expectations. What's worse, some audiences choose to trust the data visualizations without question, which can further the spread of misinformation. You can spend weeks planning your visual strategy, but **if you don't focus on visualizing data correctly at all times, that strategy won't matter.**

EXERCISE: TOP DATA VISUALIZATION MISTAKES TO AVOID

For this exercise, we'll take a look at the most common data visualization mistakes or flaws out there. To be fair, these don't include any of the issues already mentioned in this chapter. In some scenarios, there may be clear mistakes in how the data is depicted. In others, you may find that the visualization properly displays the data, but might not adhere to all best practices. As you view the visualizations that follow, try to identify why they are wrong. Once you've reviewed, flip to the Exercise Results section in this chapter to see how these visualizations should have been presented.

Lucy's Chart

Lucy is ready to report to her CEO about her team's success over the past quarter. Through new initiatives, they saw a 28-percent year-over-year increase in sales. In her presentation, she has chosen to show her success using the visualization in Figure 10.9. Can you identify what's wrong with her choice?

Figure 10.9

Charlie's Bar Graph

Charlie wants to show the value of his search-engine optimization (SEO) services so he can market his agency to new clients. His goal is to land more clients that are looking for link-building services, so he wants to show comparative data depicting his average backlinks versus his competitors'. Through some sleuthing, he's learned that competitor X averages 1,500 backlinks per client campaign. That's far less than Charlie's average of 2,300 backlinks. Competitor Y averages 2,150 backlinks per client and competitor Z averages 1,900 backlinks per client. Figure 10.10 shows how he visualized this information. What is his mistake?

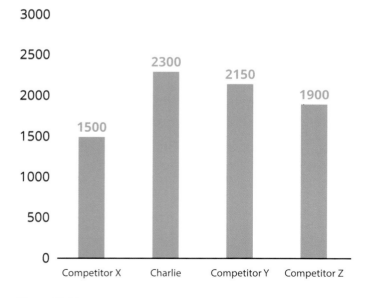

Figure 10.10

Josh's Survey

Josh has the results of a survey that he'd like to publish in order to help grow his company's thought leadership. And one data set stands out from the rest. When his core customers were asked about their upcoming challenges for the new quarter, their responses all suggested that his IT consulting services were in demand. Of 2,000 respondents who were asked to identify all answers that applied to them, he found the following:

▸ 42% felt their IT team needed an overhaul.

▸ 56% felt that their cybersecurity needs were being ignored.

▸ 17% stated that they were uncertain about the future of IT in their company.

▸ 34% said that they had ample budgets, but needed a trusted partner to use that budget with.

To show off these results, he created the data visualization in Figure 10.11. What is wrong with this graph?

34% said that they had ample budgets, but needed a trusted partner to use that budget with

42% felt their IT team needed an overhaul

Customers' upcoming challenges

17% stated that they were uncertain about the future of IT in their company

56% felt that their cybersecurity needs were being ignored

Figure 10.11

Marli's Coffee Shop

Marli has just finished designing an informational asset to share in an email marketing campaign for her coffee shop. The campaign has been set up to target current customers by showing how they have positively impacted her coffee shop throughout the year. Because current customers are the primary audience, the design incorporates her brand colors for ease of brand recognition. The data she decided to share includes:

▸ Because of customers like you, we've already achieved 75% of our giving goals this year!

▸ Our loyal customers say that 40% of their purchases are for our custom drinks.

▸ 82% of our customers visit multiple times per week.

Take a look at Figure 10.12 to see the final piece Marli designed. What seems off to you?

82% of our customers visit multiple times a week.

Because of customers like you, we have already achieved **75%** of our giving goals this year!

Our loyal customers say that **40%** of their purchases are for our custom drinks.

Figure 10.12

Andrew's Quantagram

While working on a trifold brochure for a client of his, Andrew was asked to show the client's large fleet of trucks serving customers around the country. With more than 2,500 trucks on the road in any given day, his client could easily outperform competitors, and he wanted to make sure this was shown in a compelling way.

A common way of showing off a large quantity of a single item is the quantagram. A quantagram uses icons (or pictograms) and displays them in a repeated pattern to signal a quantity of something. Quantity + Pictogram = Quantagram. Excited to show off his client's fleet, Andrew quickly created the quantagram in Figure 10.13. What was his mistake?

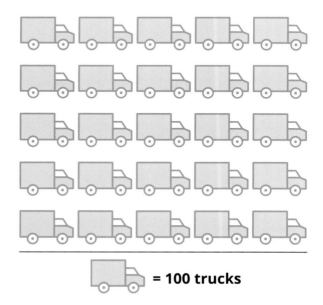

= 100 trucks

Figure 10.13

EXERCISE RESULTS: HOW TO CORRECT DATA VISUALIZATION MISTAKES

Lucy's Chart

More often than not, when we need to visualize a percentage, a pie chart is the best way to do so—and this would have been a great choice if the data Lucy wanted to represent was a portion of 100 percent. But Lucy is trying to show that her team's sales grew by 28 percent. By representing this as a pie chart, it implies that Lucy's sales were a portion of a larger whole—but they're not.

To best represent this data, Lucy needs to first show where sales were during the same time period in the previous year, then compare that number to sales in the current year. Figure 10.14 shows how to best represent this data.

28% Year-Over-Year Increase in Sales

Figure 10.14

When it comes to a percentage as a data point, it should always be visualized. In fact, this is one of the easiest forms of data to show rather than to represent through typography. When showing a percentage increase or decrease, though, never use a pie chart. Instead, always choose a bar graph that compares the increased or decreased number to the original amount from which the growth or decline stemmed.

Charlie's Bar Graph

While Charlie was right in producing a bar chart to showcase this data, he missed a clear opportunity to further his story and truly shed light on his value. Bar charts are made to be read from left to right, making the first and the final bars the most dynamic points that our eyes settle on. Since Charlie wants to show that he dominates his competition, he should order the pie chart from lowest to highest (Figure 10.15; see also Figure 10.16).

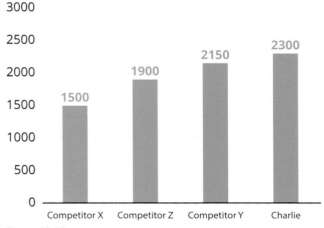

Figure 10.15

Order data from smallest to largest or largest to smallest...

... unless the x-axis or y-axis forces an order

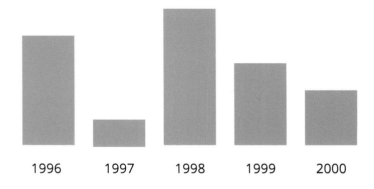

Figure 10.16

Josh's Survey

Josh was correct that pie charts should be used to show these percentages. But his respondents were given the opportunity to choose as many options as they wanted, rather than just one. Because of this, the answers add up to more than 100 percent, and a pie chart should never exceed 100 percent. The proper execution of this data would instead be to show four pie charts, preferably in order of largest to smallest or smallest to largest, as in Figure 10.17.

What if Josh had asked his respondents to choose just one answer out of a list of options? In that case, he could visualize the results in a single pie chart. With only four answers, that would be fine, but if a pie chart has more than seven slices, it becomes very confusing to the eye. So be sure to keep your pie charts under seven slices.

And when filling in each slice, pretend the chart is a clock and start at twelve o'clock. Then order your slices from largest to smallest or smallest to largest (Figure 10.18).

Customers' upcoming challenges

 56% felt that their cybersecurity needs were being ignored

 42% felt their IT team needed an overhaul

 34% said that they had ample budgets, but needed a trusted partner to use that budget with

17% stated that they were uncertain about the future of IT in their company

Figure 10.17

Always progress pie charts clockwise

Figure 10.18

Marli's Coffee Shop

Marli made some good choices with her pie charts. She ensured that they were three separate charts, put them in proper order, and started at twelve o'clock on her fill. But by using a lighter color as the fill color, it's not always clear which slice of the pie she's trying to represent. For example, when looking at the 75-percent chart, one might think that it's meant to represent 25 percent simply because the darker color is representing 25 percent.

While this is a subtle mistake, remember rule 2: small visual cues have a large impact. When you fill a glass with coffee, you can immediately see what part of that glass is "filled" with that coffee. These patterns in life should persist in design. By always choosing a darker color in your palette as the "fill" color for your data visualizations, you'll ensure that your audience will comprehend your information more easily (Figure 10.19). See the corrected visualization in Figure 10.20.

Additionally, in an attempt to get every brand color into the design, Marli changed fill colors for one of the pie charts. This disrupts the viewer and forces them to reset their expectations. When done in a singular piece of content, a change like this can impact ease of comprehension and should be avoided whenever possible.

82% of our customers visit multiple times a week.

Because of customers like you, we have already achieved **75%** of our giving goals this year!

Our loyal customers say that **40%** of their purchases are for our custom drinks.

Figure 10.19

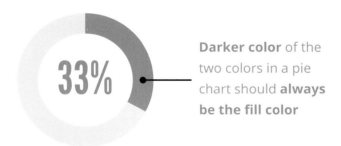

33%

Darker color of the two colors in a pie chart should **always be the fill color**

Figure 10.20

In both Josh's and Marli's cases, they could have also chosen to show their data in a single bar graph. This is often a solution when too many pie charts feel redundant or when the information deserves equal visual weight. If this is ever a consideration, keep in mind that it's still important to show a 100-percent scale to compare the data points to, as shown in Figure 10.21.

Show 100% benchmark if graph is being used to show a percentage of something.

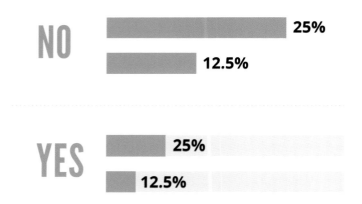

Figure 10.21

Andrew's Quantagram

Quantagrams have become an overused and almost dated form of data visualization, but they have their place. They can often be used to show volume when no other data representation will do, but they should be used sparingly and only in situations where you can show a one-to-one ratio.

In the case of Andrew's quantagram, he would have had to include 2,500 truck icons on a single page to show a true one-to-one ratio. Because he was designing a trifold brochure, this would certainly have hindered the overall design, giving far too much visual weight to a single data point. If this were the most important data point, then providing more visual weight is a good decision, but asking viewers to count every truck in the design just to glean this data is not realistic. While Andrew tried to solve this problem by showing only twenty-five truck icons with a key, that still puts the onus on the viewer to do extra math.

Only use a quantagram as a **1:1 ratio.**

If you cannot clearly visualize a stat any other way, **use typography or tie it to a related icon/illustration.**

Figure 10.22

Quantagrams should be used sparingly, and only when there isn't an alternative solution to visualize the information. If the number is greater than one hundred and a quantagram is still the only way to visualize it, then use typography to showcase the data point instead (Figure 10.22). This is one of the few times when typography is a better option than traditional forms of visualizing data.

Key Takeaway Data visualizations can help you reach new audiences and convey meaning more efficiently by transcending language and educational barriers. It makes good sense to visualize your data whenever possible. Just make sure you're doing it correctly.

The examples in this exercise are just a small sampling of common data visualization mistakes found in content marketing today. Ineffective data visualization inevitably leads to one or more of a few possible outcomes: your audience either has to work unnecessarily hard to understand what you're trying to say; misinterprets the information; or loses trust in your brand entirely. Given that the whole point of data visualization is to make information easier to understand, weak execution just won't do.

CHAPTER 11
RULE 8: COMMIT TO THE TRUTH AND PROVE IT

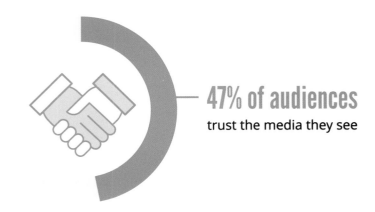

47% of audiences trust the media they see

Figure 11.1
Source: Edelman, "2019 Edelman Trust Barometer Special Report."

During the 2016 United States presidential election, the term "fake news" entered the vernacular of citizens throughout the country and around the world. While fake news has been around for centuries, it exploded during the election and was weaponized in ways that few could have predicted. The combination of a divisive campaign, ease of access to news via social-media channels, and our voracious demand for visual content created the perfect storm for fake news to flourish.

Prior to 2016, many of us were not prone to question the veracity of the visual content we were exposed to. If a photo appeared with a quote next to it, people rarely debated whether the quotation could really be attributed to the person in the photo. Instead, the visual was trusted and shared widely.

In the same vein, many believed that they would be able to spot a fake video from a mile away. Live-action video was considered a true representation of reality—unless labeled otherwise, of course. The concept of a "deepfake"—wherein artificial neural networks are used to map the likeness of another person onto an existing video, co-opting the words and facial movements from that original video in the process—was unknown to most.

But during the 2016 election, Cambridge Analytica, the Russian government, and other political actors and organizations took advantage of our blind faith in visual content. Over the course of a few short months, hundreds of thousands of fake ads were released online, inciting viral outrage among some and widespread approval among others.

The same held true for news stories. Headlines created to attract clicks often appeared alongside photos that pushed the narrative forward. This happened regardless of the true context behind said photos. Meanwhile, headlines often failed to reflect the content of the articles to which they were attached. This led to the spread of misinformation, with people only skimming headlines before moving onto their next bite-sized piece of visual content.

Beyond the headlines, memes devoured Facebook feeds. False quotes were attributed to political rivals, placed on top of unflattering photos, and trusted without question. Somehow, the simple combination of a real photo with false text made the information entirely believable. Incorrect statistics were shared widely, even as people ignored the source of that information. For those who had already decided which candidate they were going to support, these images fueled their own confirmation bias, rooting them in their choice.

To encourage distrust in the US political system, fake videos showing faulty voting machines spread across the internet like wildfire. To incite mutual fear across the political aisle, stock footage of riots was cut together with real footage of protests, suggesting that both sides were violent and unhinged. And because it was live-action video, people believed it.

Behind all of this content, multiple powers were at play, but it has been widely confirmed that Russian-government actors and the now-defunct political consultancy, Cambridge Analytica, helped to lead the charge. While Russia seemingly worked on its own, Cambridge Analytica was hired by Donald Trump's campaign to help get him elected president.

Reports show that Cambridge Analytica had access to years' worth of Facebook user data, which allowed them to build psychological profiles on potential voters, called "psychographic" profiles. By applying the rule of standing out at the cocktail party, the team at Cambridge Analytica got to know their audience very well. From there, they created hundreds of thousands of ads, memes, videos, and online experiences for several political campaigns that were uniquely catered to each individual voter profile. For instance, during the 2014 campaign to elect Thom Tillis of North Carolina, if Cambridge Analytica had identified you as "neurotic," you would see a very different ad than if they had concluded you were "open" or "agreeable," as business publication *Quartz* explains. If they could tell that someone was a single-issue voter, they delivered memes and data visualizations surrounding only that issue while implying that it was equally important to their candidate.

According to the Trump campaign, Cambridge Analytica was only used only to connect with their base and ensure they were listening to their constituents. They assert that psychographics were not a part of their tactics, the *New York Times* reports. This chapter is not intended to be an argument for or against this statement. Whether the targeted content was delivered by Cambridge Analytica or Russia doesn't matter when considering the lessons of this chapter. What matters instead is how the content was used and how well it worked.

Visual content has an immense power to persuade and dissuade audiences. When used irresponsibly, it easily rivals any propaganda published during the two world wars. We have come to rely on visual content to make information easier to comprehend and share, but the 2016 election showed the world what a volatile atmosphere visual media can help to create. And in the years since, a divide has grown between those whom global communications firm Edelman has defined as the "informed public" when compared to the mass population (see Figure 11.2).

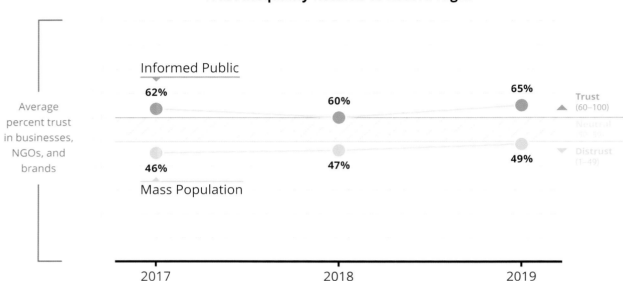

Trust Inequality Returns to Record Highs

Figure 11.2
Source: Edelman, "2019 Edelman Trust Barometer."

Who Is the "Informed Public"?

According to Edelman, the "informed public" is comprised of people who meet the following four criteria:

• Aged 25–64.

• In the top 25 percent of household income for their age group.

• College-educated.

• Report high levels of media consumption as well as engagement with business news and public policy.

Distrust in information sources has driven a deep divide between communities on a global scale, and the term "fake news" is now commonplace for us all. As a result, many organizations are feeling the sting. As citizens lose trust and faith in their government and news sources, they are putting the same microscope on brands.

TRUST IN BRANDS CONTINUES TO DECLINE

Today, businesses of all sizes are losing the faith of their customers. For example, consumers are more apt to believe their friends than they are a

Brand Trust Ranks as a Top Buying Consideration

Percent who say each is a deal-breaker or deciding factor in their buying decision

Product attributes	Quality	85
	Convenience	84
	Value	84
	Ingredients	82
	I must be able to trust the brand to do what is right.	81
Brand and company attributes	Supply chain	79
	Customer before profits	78
	Good reviews	77
	Reputation	73
	Values	72
	Environmental impact	71

Figure 11.3
Source: Edelman, "Edelman Trust Barometer Special Report."

brand when researching a product or service. In fact, findings from Nielsen's Harris Poll Online suggest that 82 percent of consumers ask for recommendations from family and friends when they're looking to purchase a product or service. And two-thirds of consumers say they're more likely to make a purchase after a recommendation via email or social media.

As today's consumers reconsider brand loyalty, an organization's commitment to the truth should be a top priority. In Edelman's 2019 trust barometer report, 67 percent of respondents agreed with the statement: "A good reputation may get me to try a product, but unless I come to trust the company behind the product, I will soon stop buying it."

In addition, with 81 percent of buyers saying that they need to trust a brand to do what's right (Figure 11.3), it's become clear that today's audiences are moved by a brand's societal impact. And with only 34 percent of consumers saying they actually trust most of the brands they use or purchase from to meet their expectations, it's clear that many organizations have a long way to go.

With this shroud of doubt surrounding many organizations, it still amazes me when visual content is released without the inclusion of a source list. Often, visual marketers and designers focus so much on creating a great piece of visual content that they feel that including references to sources would hinder the content's aesthetic success. But organizations have an uphill battle in front of them, and all media is now under scrutiny. **To succeed in the age of fake news, brands must commit to always delivering the truth as well as correctly sourcing their content so they can lead with transparency.**

EXERCISE: PROPERLY SOURCING INFORMATION

When I'm asked about the role each team member plays in creating great visual content, people are often surprised to hear that the designer should not also have the responsibility of researching or writing the content for the pieces they produce. Instead, great visual content requires the involvement of at least two individuals: a designer who can execute with visual communication as their foundation and a writer who can research primary sources while developing a narrative relevant to the brand and target audience.

This isn't at all to suggest that some designers aren't capable of doing both, but when working to deliver something accurate and high-quality, it's best to keep these roles separate. There are multiple reasons for this. For example, sometimes designers tasked with research will seek out data points that are easier to visualize, but that may not be the most impactful for the end audience. Other times, if designers are asked to research content, they may favor a narrative that allows for certain design elements without even realizing their bias.

By having a writer with a background in research and creative writing build the narrative for any piece of visual content, they act as the gatekeeper of truth. Great writers take pride in delivering content that can't be debunked. They seek out original, trustworthy sources and provide important context that will guide designers. When a writer works in tandem with a designer, the narrative takes equal priority to design, ensuring that no corners will be cut to get to a final deliverable.

Anyone producing visual content, whether it be the writer, designer, marketer, etc., needs to appreciate the value of a well-sourced and accurate storyline. Because of this, exploring how to research and source your narrative is something everyone should do, no matter what role they play in producing visual content.

A great deal of successful visual content relies on data to hook audiences and justify claims. While visualizing data correctly is extremely important for maintaining viewer confidence, properly sourcing that data is equally important. But if you're not used to researching content, you might not realize the effort required to do this correctly.

For this exercise, you will be tasked with building a narrative around the topic of coffee and tea consumption in the United States. Imagine you have a client that wants to pit coffee and tea against each other in an ultimate showdown. They own a large chain of coffee and tea shops around the country and have found that their customers are either coffee or tea enthusiasts, but rarely both. Knowing that they can inspire conversation around the differences between these two drinks, they want to create a poster for their stores and on social media. They don't want the poster to be divisive and don't want to come across like they themselves have a preference for coffee or tea.

Step 1: Determine How Client Needs Impact the Story You'll Tell

Now that these priorities have been identified, take a moment to consider how they impact the narrative. Here are a few key considerations that should drive your research:

▸ Since the coffee shop doesn't want a divisive piece, it's important for the content to provide information on coffee and tea equally. It's also important to end the piece without a conclusive statement of preference.

▸ Since this piece will be used on social media and as a poster, you'll need to keep it short and to the point. Customers won't have a lot of time to spend reviewing the poster while in line for a drink, and attention spans are short on social media. Developing a piece of content that has quick takeaways will be key.

▸ To ensure the coffee shop doesn't come across as preferential, only the facts should be provided. This means that the narrative should focus primarily on delivering data points.

Step 2: Develop an Outline Driven by Curiosity

Once these factors are considered, you will want to make an outline for your research. To do this, consider what questions matter most to you on the topic. If you were the target audience, what information would be most appealing to you? Some examples may include:

▸ How many people buy coffee in the United States and how many buy tea?

▸ What are the health benefits of coffee versus tea?

▸ What is the breakdown of those who drink their coffee or tea with cream versus those who don't?

▸ How many people prefer their coffee or tea iced?

Step 3: Find Answers to Your Questions

Once you have your list of questions, it's time to start researching answers. To do this, use some Google search tricks. Let's start with the first question, asking how many people buy coffee versus tea in the United States. At the time of this publication, a simple search with the phrase "coffee vs tea consumption in the US" yields more than forty-seven million results. The first result, however, seems quite promising (Figure 11.4).

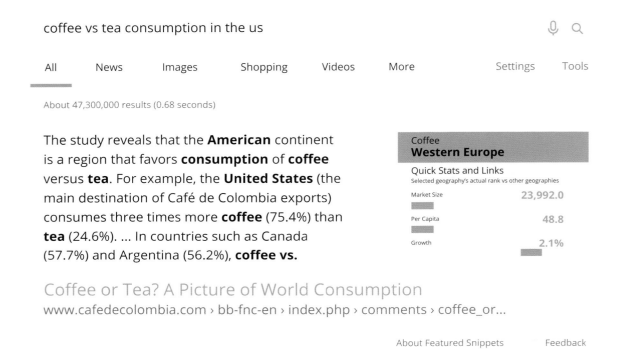

Figure 11.4

Upon clicking on the CafeDeColumbia.com link, though, it quickly becomes clear that the data is from 2014. Leading with older data is OK, if there isn't anything more current that exists. But before settling on this source, it's important to ensure there isn't anything more recent out there, since it could also be more accurate. To narrow your search, navigate to the "Tools" link under the Google search bar. An option called "Any time" appears, along with a dropdown menu from which you can choose a timeframe that will narrow down the results (Figure 11.5). I often choose "Past year" when doing research.

By changing the results to the past year, more accurate information may be at your fingertips. As an example, when I filter the results down to only content released in the past twelve months, I find links from better-known sources answering more than one of the questions I previously identified (Figure 11.6). Of course, just because a source is better-known doesn't mean they're reputable. It's still important to dig into a source to get more context.

Step 4: Find Primary Sources of Information Only

In the results I found, you'll see that a coffee-versus-tea consumption study was reported on by the *New*

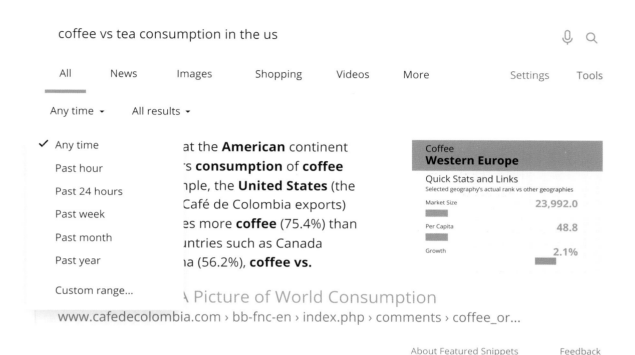

Figure 11.5

York Post. When diving into the *Post* article, it becomes clear that the study speaks to personality differences between coffee and tea drinkers. This data could serve to add humor to the narrative, but it's risky to use. The article doesn't include a link to the original source data, but does include an infographic from Chinet, the company that commissioned the study.

Since the topic for this narrative is innocent in nature, it is likely OK to report the findings of this study in the poster being produced. If this were a more hard-hitting topic, though, it would be best to seek out the original data sets and consider whether the sample size is enough to drive meaningful insights.

Luckily, there's a second result on the search engine results page that links to Statista, a great resource for gathering up-to-date data on myriad topics that always links to the primary source of information. It's important to note, though, that you have to pay for a premium account with Statista to access primary sources. If you plan to create a lot of data-driven visual content, then this investment is well worth it. When navigating to the Statista link, I'm presented with year-over-year coffee-consumption trends (Figure 11.7), and with a few clicks, I can find the original source to ensure the data is reputable.

Past year ▾   All results ▾   Clear

Oct 8, 2019 - When it comes to what goes in the hot drink of choice, coffee lovers are 96 percent more likely than tea drinkers to enjoy their brew straight. Tea fans were 35 percent more likely to have a sweet tooth and add sugar to their drinks.

Study finds the differences between coffee and tea drinkers
https://nypost.com › 2019/10/08 › study-finds-the-differences-between-cof... ▾

About Featured Snippets   Feedback

People also ask

Which is consumed more coffee or tea?   ⌄

Which has more antioxidants tea or coffee?   ⌄

How many cups of coffee a day does the average American drink?   ⌄

How much is the coffee industry worth in the US?   ⌄

Lorem ipsum

Feedback

• Total coffee per capita consumption United States, 2019 ...
https://www.statista.com › ... › Non-alcoholic Beverages
Feb 22, 2019 - We are merely doing our civil duty — after the Boston Tea Party, drinking coffee was a sign of patriotism. Since then, the popularity of coffee in the U.S. has only ...

Coffee vs. Tea: Is One Healthier Than the Other? - Healthline
https://www.healthline.com › nutrition › coffee-vs-tea
Sep 6, 2019 - The amount of caffeine considered safe for human consumption is 400 mg per day. One 8-ounce cup (240 ml) of brewed coffee contains an average of 95 mg of caffeine, compared with 47 mg in the same serving of black tea (4 , 5, 6).

57 Global Coffee Industry Statistics and Consumption Trends ...
https://foodtruckempire.com › coffee › industry-statistics

Figure 11.6

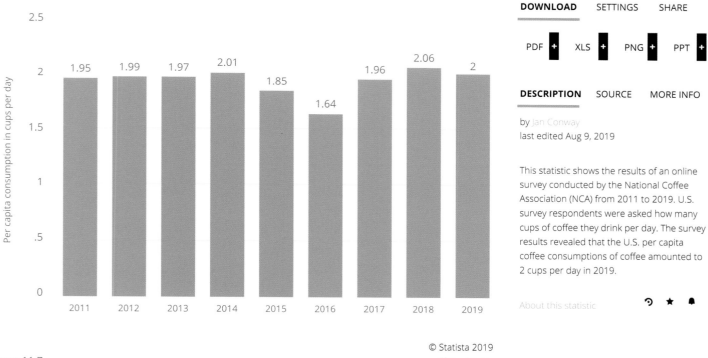

Consumer Goods & FMCG > Non-alcoholic Beverages > Total U.S. coffee per capita consumption 2011–2019

Total coffee per capita consumption in the United States from 2011 to 2019 (in cups per day)

DOWNLOAD   SETTINGS   SHARE

PDF +   XLS +   PNG +   PPT +

DESCRIPTION   SOURCE   MORE INFO

by Jan Conway
last edited Aug 9, 2019

This statistic shows the results of an online survey conducted by the National Coffee Association (NCA) from 2011 to 2019. U.S. survey respondents were asked how many cups of coffee they drink per day. The survey results revealed that the U.S. per capita coffee consumptions of coffee amounted to 2 cups per day in 2019.

About this statistic

© Statista 2019
Show source

Figure 11.7

As you dive into research like this, you'll find that some searches will deliver only partial answers. This doesn't mean that the information doesn't exist—it means that you have to get creative with your search phrases to continually uncover new data and information.

Sometimes you may luck out with a listicle of data points to help you navigate the plethora

of information sources out there. In the case of my "Past year" search results, there is an article from *Food Truck Empire* called "57 Global Coffee Industry Statistics and Consumption Trends." The article consists of compelling data points and, more importantly, links to the original sources of those data points.

When presented with content like this, it's natural to trust the article and start building your narrative from it, but try to avoid that instinct. Often, listicles may be timely, but the data may not be. Be sure to check each source to ensure that the data is truly recent and that the listicle creator presented it in the proper context.

Step 5: Always Use Reputable Sources

Taking data at face value from a secondary or tertiary source can be very risky. Just like the game of telephone, where information gets less and less accurate as it passes from one person to the next, secondary and tertiary sources don't always deliver data accurately. By finding the original source, you'll be able to understand the relevance of the information as well as how any data was gathered. This will help you get to the truth rather than furthering misinformation.

As you write your narrative, be sure to include sources for each data point you use throughout. Sources like Wikipedia and other publications that rely on the masses to self-report should be avoided. Some of the best sources include websites that end in ".gov," trusted news sources, established brands with a history of running their own studies, and peer-reviewed publications. If there's any potential that the source of information could simply be a teenager blogging in his basement, then avoid quoting that source, no matter how compelling the data is.

Step 6: Proudly Share Your Sources

Continue the steps above until you've answered all of your questions and you are confident your information sources are legitimate. This confidence is key because successful visual content always provides a list of sources for each statement of fact. Ensure your designer includes a list of sources at the bottom of any design, similar to the "Resources" section of this book. By doing so, you are displaying a commitment to the truth, which will go a long way in today's fake-news environment.

Key Takeaways The brands that expect loyalty and trust need to adjust to today's climate of fake news and uncertainty. The fact is that skepticism and cynicism go hand in hand. As audiences lose faith in media, they begin to second-guess organizations large and small. The content you produce, whether an internal or external audience, must not assume automatic trust from that audience. Instead, it's important to earn that trust by committing to the truth in all the visual content you produce and by being transparent in citing all the primary sources that informed said content.

CHAPTER 12
RULES ARE MEANT TO BE BROKEN

"Learn the rules like a pro, so you can break them like an artist."

—Pablo Picasso

The rules of visual communication should lay a strong foundation for delivering high-quality visual content for your audiences. By understanding and applying each rule, you'll find it easier to consider the subconscious effects that different design choices will have on those viewing the content.

But it is rare that every rule can be perfectly executed in every piece of content you produce, because different factors may force you to prioritize some rules over others, or even break a rule entirely. This is OK, provided that bending or breaking a rule will help you better represent the information or achieve your goals with more efficiency.

Some rules are easier to bend or break than others. For example, rule 2 (small visual cues have a large impact) and rule 7 (use proper data viz throughout) are two that I would suggest you always follow. Even in satire, breaking these rules can do more harm than good. Additionally, a rule should never be ignored simply because it's too hard to follow. Instead, each rule should be weighed in the context of the goals of the project, the information being delivered, the ways in which an audience will view the content, and the target audience. To exemplify this, here are projects from my team at Killer Visual Strategies in which we bent or broke some of the rules outlined in this book.

BREAKING RULE 1: ALWAYS THINK ABOUT CON-TEXT

The rule of con-text is usually the first to be broken when producing visual content. This makes sense, because it's far easier to let text drive meaning in visual content than it is to let the visuals themselves carry forward information. That said, this rule should never be ignored simply because it's easier to rely on text. Instead, only break this rule when it is completely impossible to visualize the information without including a little more text.

You can't simply display icons without labels for those icons; you shouldn't show a bar chart without labels and a title; and great visual content is easier to digest with headlines breaking up sections within the design. These are all times when text is needed, but even in these instances, you aren't really breaking the rule as long as your visuals represent the information clearly.

Consider a flow chart, though. Most flow charts require a series of yes-or-no questions and labels. But this doesn't mean that they're not great examples of visual communication. Before reading the questions or labels, a viewer can easily discern that they are about to experience a decision tree. The sizes and shapes of labels and boxes may even imply a pattern within the tree. Color choices might also drive the eye to conclusions. And the arrows within a flow chart set a pace and direction for the viewer. As a result, there are multiple visual cues to make the information easier to consume, even if incorporating text is necessary to help audiences along the way.

Perhaps the best example of this rule being broken lies in my favorite project ever produced by my team. When asked to create a poster showcasing the large footprint of the tech sector in Washington State (with a primary focus on the Puget Sound and Seattle areas), our team was tasked with visualizing a list of nearly 1,000 company names and their relationships to one another.

The goal of the piece was to show which companies fueled innovation and how companies were connected to one another. For example, maybe a former Microsoft employee went out on their own to start a new and successful company. Or perhaps a leader from Expedia teamed up with a leader from Amazon to build a new brand. By studying the history of founders alongside the largest names in the Pacific Northwest, we could begin to connect the dots of innovation, so to speak.

View the resulting design in Figure 12.1.

While this design is exceptionally text-heavy, it still lets visual communication guide the viewer. Text is used only for labels, because delivering the same visual with logos would create a cluttered and harder-to-navigate design. Arrows and circle treatments are used to lend meaning to the text and communicate the information visually.

Figure 12.1 [ ]

▶ Circles are used to indicate three types of companies:

  » Solid circles with dots in the center show companies that have been acquired.

  » Solid circles on their own show companies that have not been acquired.

  » Solid circles that rest inside a hashed external circle represent engineering centers. Engineering centers are companies that were founded outside of the Pacific Northwest, but have a large presence and workforce in the area.

▶ Arrows lend further meaning to the design by depicting the relationships between companies:

  » Solid arrows guide a viewer from a company where founders were previously employed to the companies they founded, thus linking innovation to key hubs like Microsoft, Amazon, the University of Washington, and others.

  » Companies with multiple founders are indicated through dotted-line arrows connecting out from the businesses the founders left to start their new businesses.

  » If a company was acquired, a dashed line connects them to the organization that acquired them.

  » The direction in which the arrow points also drives meaning. The arrow always points away from a company where someone was employed and toward the company they started.

  » In the case of acquisitions, the arrow points from the acquirer to the acquiree.

Upon initially viewing this design, one can quickly identify the largest innovation hubs in the Puget Sound region. The visualization proves their impact and value both inside and outside Seattle. Once an audience is hooked, they can spend hours mapping the connections between each company. While this poster has at least 1,000 words of text, it doesn't hurt the design in this situation. The rule of con-text has been broken, but the piece still leads with visual communication at its core.

BREAKING RULE 3: THERE'S NO GOLD AT THE END OF THAT RAINBOW

Great designers will likely look at this rule and throw it out the window immediately. While it's imperative to use color intentionally, in a way that delivers meaning wherever possible, experienced designers are able to achieve this even with a more robust color palette. If you are not a designer or are just starting out, however, it is still encouraged to follow the three-color rule.

When we started Killer Visual Strategies in 2010, our focus was mainly on infographic design (hence our original name, Killer Infographics). Much of what we were creating included data-rich designs that benefited from sticking to the three-color rule. Often, when delivering a data-rich piece of content, it's important to stick to a pattern of colors. This ensures that viewers won't read meaning into your color choices when looking at the various data visualizations. But what happens when a piece of content isn't driven by data viz? It took a year before we truly came across this dilemma, and decided to break the rule of rainbows.

We were hired to design a series of infographics for an information technology (IT) certification program. The client wanted to stand out from his competitors, who were providing potential students with data-rich arguments about the benefits of a degree in IT. But in our client's opinion, if someone was already looking at a certification program, they probably knew the benefits. Instead, our client wanted to appeal to students on a more personal level. He wanted to show off his brand's personality by making students laugh. He also wanted to gain backlinks to the program website by creating something that would inspire debate and conversation.

These priorities inspired "Geek vs. Nerd," the first infographic in what would become a series. Figure 12.2 shows an excerpt of the design, the piece that acted as the visual hook.

The design went viral within days of its release. While some agreed with the differentiators between geeks and nerds, a small subset of the population was wholly offended. A pattern emerged in which people claimed that some of the traits called out in the infographic should in fact apply to "hipsters" rather than geeks. This inspired the second infographic in the series, "Geek vs. Hipster" (excerpted in Figure 12.3).

The "versus" series continued with "Seattle Geek vs. Silicon Valley Geek" (excerpted in Figure 12.4) and "Guy Kawasaki vs. Seth Godin" (excerpted in Figure 12.5; see also Figures F.1 and F.2).

As you can see in all of these examples, myriad colors are used to bring the content to life. In each case, illustrated scenes of people are shown and colors help to bring important details to life. In the case of "Seth Godin vs. Guy Kawasaki," the dominant purple choice for Godin and the dominant red for Kawasaki was very intentional. At the time, Godin was best known for his book, *Purple Cow* (which sported a purple cover with cow spots), while Kawasaki was best known for his book, *Enchantment* (which had a red cover with a butterfly).

As you can see, in all of these examples, the rule of rainbows was ignored. Despite this, colors were used with great intent. In each case, the designer chose a dominant color to connect with each topic, and carried that color forward throughout the design.

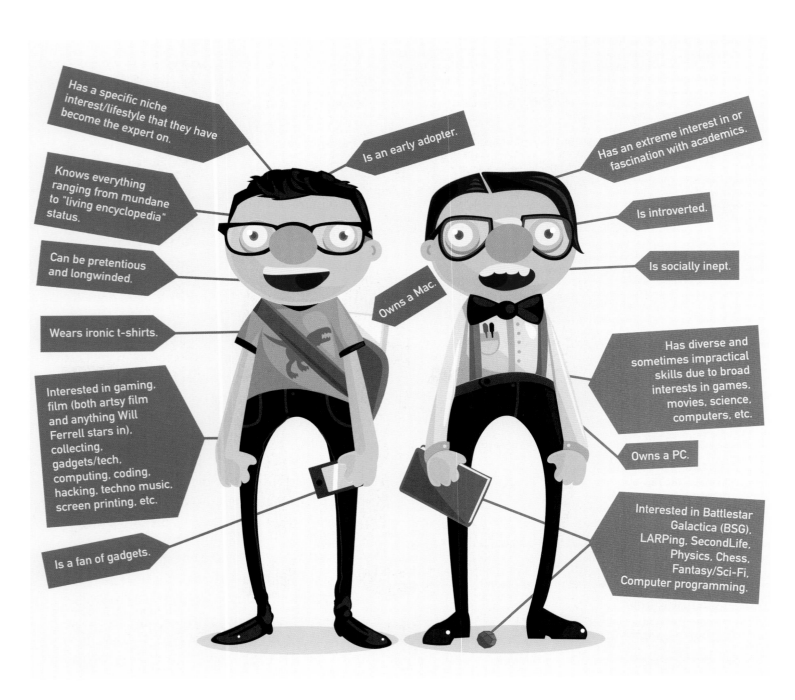

Has a specific niche interest/lifestyle that they have become the expert on.

Knows everything ranging from mundane to "living encyclopedia" status.

Can be pretentious and longwinded.

Wears ironic t-shirts.

Interested in gaming, film (both artsy film and anything Will Ferrell stars in), collecting, gadgets/tech, computing, coding, hacking, techno music, screen printing, etc.

Is a fan of gadgets.

Is an early adopter.

Owns a Mac.

Has an extreme interest in or fascination with academics.

Is introverted.

Is socially inept.

Has diverse and sometimes impractical skills due to broad interests in games, movies, science, computers, etc.

Owns a PC.

Interested in Battlestar Galactica (BSG), LARPing, SecondLife, Physics, Chess, Fantasy/Sci-Fi, Computer programming.

Figure 12.2 [ ]

Figure 12.3 [ ]

Figure 12.4 [ ]

Figure 12.5 [ ]

BREAKING RULE 4: GOOD VISUAL STRATEGISTS ASK "WTF?!"

While fonts carry forward meaning, oftentimes a brand requires that its fonts be used in all of its content. This can be difficult for any designer, because their creativity becomes restricted.

To put this into perspective, imagine facing a home-remodeling project where the only tools at your disposal are a screwdriver, a hammer, and a handsaw. Sure, you can likely get the job done with those tools, but a power saw and drill would be two simple additions that could greatly improve your efficiency. Fonts are tools to communicate a mindset or emotion, but what if you couldn't leverage those tools accordingly?

When working with large brands, designers might find that sticking to their fonts is often more important than deviating from them to deliver a larger impact. This has been true for the Global 2000 companies we have worked with for years. To maintain quality standards within very large organizations, restricting communicators to a specific set of fonts is a must.

When a brand forces their fonts on a design, it should never be a deal-breaker. Instead, it should be embraced as a challenge while font weights and sizes should act as the solution to that challenge. In other words, while your toolbox is light, how you wield those tools makes a big difference.

To exemplify this, consider a series of assets we designed for a client with Lexia as their primary brand font. Take a look at the screenshots from key scenes, shown in Figures 12.6–12.8. You'll see that this font is elevated by the designer through size differences, color choices, and bolder weights where appropriate.

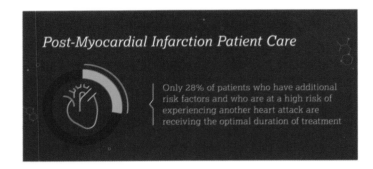

Figure 12.6

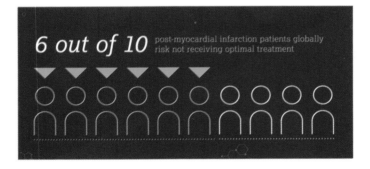

Figure 12.7

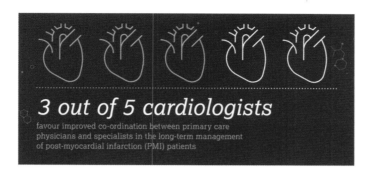

Figure 12.8

As you can see based on subtle visual cues in the design, this client lives in the world of science and medicine. Their brand font choice communicates an authority and professionalism that works well for their industry. So it makes sense that all vendors must adhere to these brand choices, despite the fact that it breaks the WTF rule. When forced to break this rule yourself, consider how font sizes, colors, and weights can be used to elevate font choices and draw the eye into key points.

BREAKING RULE 5: AVOID THE STIGMA OF STOCK

Chapter 8 offers multiple tips on how to use stock imagery if you are unable to use anything else. But other times, you may find that you don't need to break the rule, but that doing so will add efficiencies without hindering the overall success of your end deliverable.

To exemplify this, consider the illustration in Figure 12.9, excerpted from a design we created at Killer called "Are You Working Your Employees to Death?"

While the illustration is very compelling and acts as a great visual hook for the audience, it was also quite time-intensive to produce. Would this piece have lost its value if the stock image in Figure 12.10 were used instead?

Figure 12.9 [ ]

Figure 12.10

Figure 12.11

By adding filters and properly framing this photo within the design, you could still ensure the infographic packs a powerful punch. It may not be as engaging as a custom illustration, but it can work in a pinch if you have time or budget constraints.

In the context of editorial design, stock imagery can have even more of a place than custom illustration. Editorial design typically comes in the form of PowerPoint presentations, white papers, e-books, blog posts, and multipage reports. Great editorial design contains a healthy mix of slides or sections driven by visual communication and other segments primarily dedicated to long-form text.

When developing content like this, it often helps to break up the long-form text with photography because iconography, data visualizations, or illustration may not feel appropriate to the content. I'd still encourage you to use custom photography over stock imagery, but I know that it's rare for small and mid-sized organizations to have their own collection of custom photos.

Figure 12.12

Check out Figures 12.11–12.13 to see a few examples of how stock photography can be used within editorial design to keep the viewer engaged.

As you can see, there are times when this rule can be bent or broken, but applying unique filters and framing to your stock photos can go a long way toward making them feel custom and original.

BREAKING RULE 6: STAND OUT AT THE COCKTAIL PARTY

"My target audience is everyone!" This is what one of my clients exclaimed when I shared the rule of standing out at a cocktail party. Sometimes company goals or budgets greatly restrict the ability to create content geared toward specific target audiences. In other words, it's not always easy to stand out at a cocktail party. There are cases in which you might make a group announcement in the hopes that

Figure 12.13

Figure 12.14

enough people have stopped their conversations long enough to listen.

When delivering content geared toward the Everyman, it's important to make safe choices. This happened for our team at Killer in 2014 when a team at the National Endowment for the Arts (NEA) hired us to revamp their visual identity and build a five-year content campaign. At the time, they were entering their fiftieth year of service to the arts community and needed a partner to help them make inroads with new donors and constituents, and to ensure another fifty years of success.

As an agency, we were tasked with building a visual language that would speak equally to a donor base older than forty-five, legislators in Washington, and younger generations who had not heard of the NEA or didn't understand its value. See what we created in Figure 12.14.

This visual language seems simple at first, but every single design choice ensured equal treatment of each target audience. Consider the following distinctions:

▸ The color palette is intentionally broad. It is Americans with Disabilities Act–accessible, which is required by any government organization. What's more, it includes a variety of colors so that they can be applied based on which segment of the NEA's broad audience each asset is speaking to. When a topic would matter more to a legislator than a millennial, for example, more muted tones from the color palette can be used to let the information be the star of the design.

▸ The font choice is modern, thin, and sans serif. This speaks equally to all audiences, but the thin font choice ensures that it can be taken seriously by a more mature viewer.

▸ The data visualization style is intentionally simplified. When communicating important information to government officials, it's important to lead with authority. By sticking to traditional charts and graphs, we ensure that nothing feels convoluted or misrepresented. Meanwhile, the use of donut pie charts instead of traditional pie charts lends the content a modern look that attracts younger viewers.

▸ Character illustrations are purposely faceless. By choosing this detailed silhouette style, character illustrations can be easily altered to represent various demographics, across both age and race. In addition, the lack of facial expression ensures no viewer is alienated when viewing characters that may be intended to represent them.

When you're forced to break the rule of standing out at the cocktail party, you can still make smart design decisions that ensure flexibility and speak equally to a variety of viewers.

BREAKING RULE 8: COMMIT TO THE TRUTH AND PROVE IT

You may be wondering why some rules were omitted from this chapter when this rule—about something as important as always committing to the truth—was not. The term "fake news" has broad implications—to such an extent that it has become a catch-all phrase often used for political gain. Should a government official want to ignore some fact, they can publicly defame reports of said fact as "fake news." This has led to a black-and-white view of information and content that deserves to be challenged.

In the October 2019 issue of *American Behavioral Scientist*, researchers from Penn State University categorized fake news into seven distinct buckets: false news, polarized content, misreporting, commentary, persuasive information, citizen journalism, and satire. To juxtapose these, they noted that trustworthy content follows journalistic standards such as citing reputable primary sources and adhering to a grammatically correct, impartial, and authoritative written style.

It's easy to find examples of powerful visual content across all seven buckets of fake news. But to maintain the trust of your audience, it is highly encouraged that you avoid creating content that could be categorized as false news, polarized content, misreporting, and citizen

Figure 12.15 [ ]

journalism. That being said, there is a prominent place for satire, persuasive information, and commentary in visual content that should be embraced rather than avoided.

Explainer videos, which often tell the story of a brand product or service in less than ninety seconds, are a great example of persuasive information. A good explainer video will include data points from external and reputable sources, but may often include claims from the company behind the video as well.

When the Killer team produced a motion graphic for our friends at the Happy Egg Company, a free-range egg brand, the script we wrote included the claim that "happy hens like to look good" along with a variety of

other assumptions surrounding the preferences of a "happy hen." (You can view a screenshot from that video in Figure 12.15, or watch the full motion graphic at bit.ly/HappyEggVideo.)

Of course, who actually knows whether hens feel happiness? Should this motion graphic be considered untrustworthy as a result? The simple answer is no. This video may take creative liberties, but it was made as both a persuasive form of content and entertainment. Because it was packaged as such, the audience expects to willingly suspend disbelief during the 65-second run time.

Visual content also acts as a great vessel for satire and commentary. The infographic "versus" series I referred to earlier in this chapter is a great example of satire mixed with commentary. While, yes, some well-sourced data points complement the caricatures in each design, there isn't a reputable source out there that would claim to know the exact characteristics of a geek, nerd, or hipster.

Pop Chart, whose "Insanely Great History of Apple" poster I talked about in chapter 9, delivers an abundance of satire within the infographic posters its team develops. Some of the best include their "Alphabet of Animal Professions" and their "Periodic Table of Hip-Hop."

When breaking rule 8, it's important to make it obvious to your audience that you're working within the realm of satire or commentary. Applying a journalistic style implies the content should be taken seriously. This may backfire if the topic is too believable, as it did for Orson Welles when his dramatized reading of *The War of the Worlds* on live radio in 1938 caused widespread panic.

To ensure your content is viewed as satire or commentary, consider using a more conversational tone within the text of the content. Choose a title that is obviously humorous or incorporate modern slang within the piece. If it still doesn't seem clear, be sure to label your content as commentary or satire to ensure your audience doesn't misinterpret your intent.

Key Takeaways The rules of visual communication exist to provide guidance on developing successful visual content, but they do not have to be taken so seriously that you never bend or break them. When determining which rules matter most, you should always weigh them against the goals of your content, your target audience, and the information you are trying to share. Sometimes you'll find that adhering too strictly to a rule will alienate your audience, misrepresent your information, or run counter to the goals you are hoping to achieve. If this is the case, let the rule act as a guidepost only, but don't go out of your way to make it your North Star.

PART THREE:
YOUR VISUAL STRATEGY

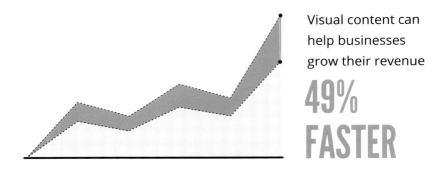

Visual content can help businesses grow their revenue

49% FASTER

Figure P3.1
Source: Aberdeen Group and Vidyard, "The Impact of Video Marketing."

When I founded Killer Visual Strategies in 2010, the landscape of creative services was drastically evolving. While the large agencies of the world had become accustomed to equally large retainers and had grown complacent about the future ahead, the tide was changing.

Access to skilled services was no longer locked behind the walls of the agency elite. Talent pools were abundant and no longer restricted by geographic location, making it easy to find affordable and gifted designers. Meanwhile, thanks to the wide adoption of video conferencing, large brands had stopped expecting in-person meetings before choosing a vendor. This made it possible for small shops to compete without the expense of travel and pitch decks.

The combination of traditional pricing models, extensive overhead, and sizable staffs made it hard for seasoned agencies to course-correct fast enough. They appeared bloated and overpriced while freelancers and small agencies provided competitive rates, dedicated attention, and speedy delivery. Seasoned agencies began losing work to fledgling firms that seemed to appear overnight. Traditional firms were hurting, small teams were beginning to make headway, and organizations of all sizes were caught in the middle.

The economy was rebounding from the 2008 financial crisis, but not fast enough. At the same time, savvy marketers knew that customer demand for engaging content would only continue to grow. To keep up with that demand while the purse strings were tight, they turned to freelancers and newly launched small firms for help. For freelancers, this was the dawn of the gig economy. For small shops like mine, it was an opportunity to become something more than a lifestyle business.

But this flurry of options for organizations looking to produce visual content has also led to an abundance of subpar providers. And while consumers demand quality, content creators wrestle with shoestring budgets. As a result, inferior content has become the norm, with organizations expecting to create competitive media for just pennies on the dollar. When that media fails, they often blame the content rather than the process, budget, or level of skill that their budget allowed for.

Anyone seeking to develop a successful visual strategy must learn to choose wisely from among the plethora of content creators. While the first two parts of this book have laid a foundation for identifying and producing quality work, successful visual content can only be created with the right team executing on a solid process.

If it's your job to put a team and process in place, the pages that follow will outline the necessary steps for you to do just that. You'll discover how to leverage your options to find the right creatives for the right tasks, whether that means working with freelancers, in-house teams, or agencies. You'll learn how to surround yourself with the right team and identify true visual communicators. And you'll explore several different processes for creating great visual content.

If you are a content creator yourself, part 3 of this book will help you build a process that works for both you and your end clients. You'll learn where you fit into that process as well as where you may need to bring in partners who can contribute to a successful strategy. And you'll gain insight into the rates you can command when producing quality work.

Technological innovations and cultural shifts will continue to challenge the status quo. To deliver the best visual strategy, you'll need to prepare yourself for the future of visual content. And that is where this book concludes: with a prediction of what's to come, so you can build upon the lessons in this book and be ready for what comes next.

CHAPTER 13

YOU CAN'T CREATE GREAT CONTENT WITHOUT A GREAT TEAM AND PROCESS

> *"I believe in people, process, and product. I can improve the product, we can work on the process. But sometimes you just can't change the people."*

—*Marcus Lemonis*
"The Profit"

For the agencies that launched shortly after the economic crisis in 2008, one thing was certain: generalist firms could not withstand the shifting economy. Instead, providing a niche service would not only ensure an agency could hold its own among larger brands, but when combined with a great process and a talented team, it would help them thrive into the future.

Creative teams of all types rise and fall because of process and talent. Being strong in one arena is not enough to ensure consistent success. Whether you are serving the internal needs of your organization, driving strategy while partnering with a creative team, or developing content for clients, it's imperative that you center your visual strategy around both talent and process equally.

CREATING GREAT VISUAL CONTENT IS LIKE BUILDING A HOUSE

Consider this: if you were building your dream house, would you skip interviewing architects, creating blueprints, or laying a foundation? Of course not. When making such a sizable financial and emotional investment, it's par for the course to leave no stone unturned. Yet when it comes to visual content, which can yield multimillion-dollar returns when produced correctly, we often cut corners.

While there's not a one-size-fits-all approach to developing visual content, some key steps should never be ignored. I like to compare the process of following and implementing these steps to building a house.

As you consider this process, remember that every role matters. For example, if you are a content strategist, you'll need to rely on a designer to manage some of the steps that follow. If you're a designer, you may need to depend on a strategist and a project manager to own various steps in the process. To help identify where you best fit into the process, keep your eyes peeled for the icon that best matches your role in the diagram in Figure 13.1.

Whether you're creating visual content yourself or working with a vendor, you should never skip these six steps. Great visual strategists build additional steps into their process based on the desired outcomes of the content. For example, if content is animated, then animation should start only after designs are fully approved. The steps of getting a voiceover as well as adding a score and sound design should be considered in the process as well.

FINDING YOUR CREATIVE CONTENT TEAM

Great talent drives visual strategy, but with so many options at your disposal, where do you even start to find that talent? For today's content creators, a consistent battle between in-house expertise, freelance services, and specialized agency work has become the norm. Making the wrong choice can make or break careers, while finding the right fit can catapult a brand.

This changing landscape laid the foundation on which I built my company, Killer Visual Strategies. To ensure it brings you success, as well, you must understand how to best navigate the waters.

Before you start, though, you must know that it takes a village.

It was late in September 2010 when I received our first order for an infographic design. At the time, my company was called Killer Infographics and the primary business model had nothing to do with providing design services. At best, we were critics of the medium, offering candid reviews of those who had submitted their designs to us for feedback. At worst, we were two marketers working out of my old business partner's townhome, learning about visual communication by making our own litany of mistakes.

When the request came through, I chose to take on the design work myself. We were offered $300, provided the exact word-for-word copy needed for the design, and told that we could use online templates if need be (something I would never do today). Our original business model was making only $4,000 per month, which could not sustain the Seattle mortgages both myself and my old business partner had to cover. We were offered the opportunity to

make $300 in less than a day, and I couldn't find a reason to say "no."

The first design was a success, though it was made easy by the client-provided template and data-rich content. The client saw an opportunity to get infographics both fast and cheap, while I saw an opportunity to grow our revenue and do something I loved at the same time. As a result, I spent the next few months pushing for a pivot in our business model so that we could become a specialized and nimble design firm.

Of course, we couldn't sustain a large influx of work if I was expected to continue handling a combination of sales, project management, and design all at the same time. Luckily, I knew some very talented designers who were looking for work due to the down economy and were excited for the opportunity to have some regular income. Given the low rates we were charging, the best business model to pursue at the time was one where we acted as the middlemen between clients and freelancers. We would take orders, build creative briefs, and match the work to freelancers we could trust.

While this seemed simple enough, it was anything but. We quickly learned that it was hard to find a consistent freelancer, especially if we couldn't provide consistent work. More often than not, work would be turned in late or not at all, leaving me scrambling to take on projects myself so as to ensure they wouldn't also be late to the end client. Some freelancers even tried to pass off stock vector assets as their

1

Shop Around

You wouldn't build your dream house without first shopping around for the best architect and contractor. Why would you do the same with a visual content project?

 Interview different creative teams to ensure they communicate well, are accountable, can properly deliver on the rules of visual communication, and know how to meet your goals.

 You wouldn't design and build a house all by yourself. That's why great designers should partner with great writers and project managers to provide competitive and efficient services.

 Take some time to surround yourself with people who share your values and have capabilities that exceed your own. It takes a village to create great visual content.

2

Identify Design Specs

When building a house, design specs are finalized before work begins. This ensures the project stays on budget and on schedule, and makes stakeholder expectations clear.

 For any creative project or series of projects, it's imperative to document all expectations in a creative brief before any work starts. This ensures that all key stakeholders are on the same page while giving you a tool to reign in scope if someone seeks to shift direction midway through a project.

> **Quick tip:** A good creative brief will identify the target audience as well as a singular goal for the content. This ensures that both remain top-of-mind over the course of the project.

3

Commit to a Schedule

It's a common story: you've hired a carpenter for a home repair and they show up late. Project delays can cost you both time and money.

 Wrangling a creative team can sometimes feel like organizing a construction schedule. Be clear on who you'll need, when.

 Missing deadlines costs everyone in the end, so set a schedule and cadence of deliverables up front and don't let anyone miss a deadline.

Figure 13.1

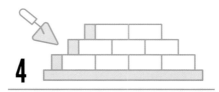

4

Lay the Foundation

You can't build a house without laying the foundation, and you can't develop great visual content if you skip important steps.

 Design can't start until the word-for-word text of the content has been set in stone.

 Your script will give the designer the necessary context to inspire creative ideas, determine a layout, and make design decisions.

 You wouldn't ask builders to add new rooms once house construction has started. So make sure the designer has all the info before they get started.

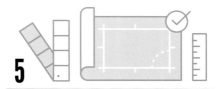

5

Finalize Blueprints and Swatches

Without blueprints, a construction crew might cut corners, forget project goals, and miss deadlines. Proper planning ensures creative teams always follow best practices.

 Mood boards are like fabric swatches, inspiring the visual aesthetic of the project. Wireframes are like blueprints, showing the expected layout for the design. Make sure you include both.

 Designers should guide all parties through the wireframe. From there, all stakeholders should weigh in on a design direction before the heavy lifting of design begins.

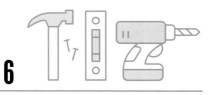

6

Build, Check In, and Keep Building

Don't start design until you've accomplished steps 1–5.

 You wouldn't commission your dream house, then disappear until it's done. Instead, you'd check in regularly.

 Great project managers provide regular updates, field questions, manage the timeline, and plan check-ins.

 Work with the designer to ensure they're visualizing the information accurately. Writers should also proof and review all designs.

 With each draft, implement changes until the requirements of the creative brief are met.

 Content Strategist    Writer/ Storyteller   Project Manager   Designer   The Whole Team

own, original artwork. Left unchecked, this could have put our clients into very precarious situations. Additionally, training designers in the best practices of visual communication seemed like an uphill battle when communicating exclusively via email and quick calls.

Four months into our pivot, though, we were averaging $40,000 per month in revenue! Even so, it was a drastic shift, and not without its many costs. In fact, we were competing on price rather than value. Our relatively cheap offerings brought in business, but that also meant that we couldn't pay our freelancers enough to do their jobs properly. Profit margins were slim, so we also couldn't hire the right staff to play the myriad roles required to create great visual content. We found ourselves at a crossroads, where we could either continue to be the fast food of infographic design or up our prices and provide our clients and their audiences with a far more palatable experience.

Exhausted by the myriad issues caused by delivering on a budget, we chose to double our prices, bring our best freelancer in-house, and hire a hybrid researcher and project manager. While this eased the pain, it didn't alleviate it all together. Over the next few months, we continued to hone our service and rework our pricing to accommodate additional needs. By the time we were finally firing on all cylinders, it had become clear that high-quality visual content required a village to produce.

Two years into our business, our team had expanded beyond infographics to all forms of visual content. We had stopped working with freelancers entirely and had a robust in-house team of visual strategists. To deliver on even small projects, we would employ creative writers and researchers, project and account managers, skilled designers, animators, and developers. As we began managing content strategy and large campaigns for our clients, we grew our marketing and strategy team, added an art director, a creative director, and other roles.

When you consider how to create your own village of experts to drive your organization's visual strategy, it's important to understand that all of these roles are crucial. If you choose to work with freelancers, you will end up having to take on many of these roles yourself. If you choose to work with an agency, it will be important to understand how they value each position as well as what they expect from you. And if you choose to build an in-house team, you'll have to find skilled talent that can lend experience where you might be lacking.

This isn't to say that you can't do it all yourself, but just like if you were building a house, being a one-person show doesn't always yield the best results. You may sacrifice timeliness, affordability, or quality—all of which will hinder the return on investment that your work can deliver. With all of this in mind, I suggest you decide between one of three paths: freelance, in-house, or agency. In the coming chapters, I'll explore these three options in-depth.

If you are a skilled designer looking to build or join a support team, you'll still want to consider how these avenues might affect you. For example, you could consider hiring a freelance project manager. Alternatively, you could be looking to become more competitive as a freelancer yourself. In either situation, the considerations outlined in Chapter 14 will still apply to you, even though that chapter mainly focuses on how a content strategist may hire a freelance designer.

You'll find that similar value can be gained by reading about the other paths one might take. So even if certain options do not directly apply to you, I encourage you to review them so you can better understand the landscape that exists for content creators of all kinds.

But in a world of possibilities, one can easily get lost in a spiral of never-ending options. Navigating the myriad possible paths toward quality visual content might seem overwhelming at best, impossible at worst. In 2010, many of those options were just beginning to emerge, whereas today, specialized firms deliver the majority of the content we all consume.

Key Takeaways

▸ When creating visual content, follow the outlined six-step process in this chapter at minimum. Build upon that process if the content calls for it.

▸ Don't try to do everything yourself. It takes a village to create great visual content at the speed at which today's audiences expect it.

▸ At minimum, your creative team should include a talented designer, writer/researcher, and project manager.

▸ Visual strategy requires strategic minds. Consider adding a creative director, art director, marketer, and other roles to your team to develop a competitive campaign.

▸ Avoid the appeal of cheap prices. For a service provider to deliver on a budget, they will have to cut corners or hire subpar talent. A low-quality project will cost you more in opportunity and reputation loss than budgeting properly to get content that will drive a great return on your investment.

CHAPTER 14
GOING THE
FREELANCE ROUTE

>50% of the US workforce is projected to consist of freelance workers by 2027

Figure 14.1
Source: Callaham, "Are You a Baby Boomer Looking for Work?"

More often than not, working with freelancers can feel like the path of least resistance when you want to develop great visual content. If you are a good communicator and project manager, then this might be the case for you. Freelancers are agile, affordable, and often willing to work evenings and weekends to ensure a fast turnaround. Because of this, they can provide organizations with immediate support when they need it most. But if you struggle with communicating your expectations, have a lot of work on your plate already, or cannot fully envision the content you want developed, then working with the wrong freelancer can do more harm than good.

When you work with most freelancers, it's important to consider that a few key roles in the development of your visual strategy will always fall on your plate, so you must be prepared to dedicate your time and attention to the project at hand. You will need to scrutinize the level of effort required of you and determine how many hours you will have to contribute to the project if you want to ensure that working with a freelancer will truly save you time and money.

At minimum, expect to take on the following responsibilities when hiring most freelancers:

▸ Determining and clearly defining the overall goals of your content or campaign.

▸ Identifying the types of content that will best meet those goals.

▸ Providing the word-for-word copy for whatever your freelancer is designing.

▸ Developing a clear creative brief.

▸ Determining a schedule and cadence of deliverables.

RATE OF PAY IMPACTS QUALITY OF SERVICE

Most freelancers agree to flat rates for projects, opting not to charge hourly in the hopes of winning the work. But the gig economy has forced onshore designers to compete with offshore talent, so freelancers often find themselves undervaluing their own services. While the rush of winning a job drives initial excitement at the start of a project, as the hours drone on, they could quickly lose interest if they don't feel that their time is being respected.

Paying your freelancer too little is a risk worth avoiding if you don't want to lose a potentially great partner. Pay your freelancer well and they will be loyal to you when urgent needs arise. Pay them too little and you may lose them midway through your project.

To determine how their hourly rate shakes out, be sure to get an hour estimate for the work needed and compare it to the flat rate. According to Eyal Bino in Forbes, the average hourly rate for freelancers is $19 per hour. To be fair, this global average is drastically reduced by offshore pricing and is rarely enough for most talented freelancers to maintain their practice. Considering this, if you're working with a United States–based freelancer, you should expect to spend at least $50 per hour to ensure they are fairly compensated.

You'll also want to be realistic about the hours needed for the level of work you've requested. Great content takes time. If you're not a designer, you'll likely assume the work takes about half the time it actually should. This is because we naturally tend to believe tasks that we don't do ourselves are simpler than they are, in the same way we can be persuaded by a get-rich-quick scheme. If it seems too good to be true, it probably is.

Quick tip: In Appendix C of this book, I provide a table of hourly rate estimates for different types of visual media. When in doubt, use it as a reference to ensure you're being charged appropriately for the work at hand.

If you are paying rates less than $45 per hour for your freelancer, you shouldn't expect them to provide services beyond execution. This isn't to say that they aren't wholly capable of delivering a strategic approach to your content needs, but instead that the associated rate calls for executing on a clearly defined vision only.

When paying these rates, you will likely need to take on further responsibilities, including:

▸ Fully managing the agreed-upon schedule, policing deliverables and timelines to ensure due dates are not missed.

▸ Managing scope to ensure your budget is spent executing on the right direction for the work.

▸ Acting as the art director by providing a thorough explanation of how you want the design to look and feel.

▸ Policing the execution to ensure it adheres to the rules of visual communication.

▸ Providing very prescriptive feedback rather than identifying problems and relying on your designer to propose solutions.

The world is filled with exceptional freelancers, but finding one can sometimes feel like searching for a needle in a haystack. Great freelancers either have a long waiting list, know their value enough to charge agency rates of $75 to $175 per hour, or are in the process of starting their own agency themselves. The value and experience they bring to the table often means that a great freelancer is worth their weight in gold.

To exemplify this, here are some key services and attributes you should expect from a freelancer charging $75 per hour or more:

▸ Freelance design should either be their full-time job, or they should commit to being available anytime during your work schedule.

▸ They should help you determine what content will best meet your goals.

▸ They should propose a schedule to you, noting points where they will need to check in with you, and identifying how they will ensure key deliverables are not missed.

▸ They should listen to your goals and walk through their design thinking, identifying solutions that will achieve your goals every step of the way.

▸ They should embrace the rules of visual communication and provide examples that display how they will adhere to those rules.

▸ They should propose a collaborative process that allows for iterations on each deliverable.

▸ Many will provide a detailed scope of work, creative brief, or both.

▸ They should have the ability to work within a range of aesthetic styles, ensuring they will be able to deliver content that brings your brand identity to life.

▸ They should discuss communication styles and expectations with you to ensure your relationship is founded on mutual accountability.

FINDING THE RIGHT FREELANCER FOR YOU

Whether you settle on a freelancer whose focus is just on execution or one who will also bring strategic thinking and management to the mix, it's imperative you choose someone you can trust. You might be impressed with their portfolio, but you don't know how much time they took to create each piece or how

much feedback was required for them to get to a final result. Instead, you have to dig deeper to ensure you can find the best freelancer for your needs.

Look for the following when trying to find the right freelancer for you:

▸ **Client history:** Check the freelancer's portfolio to see what clients they have worked with in the past. Make sure they have more than one project example from at least one of their clients. This shows that the client came back for more work. Next, check to see if you recognize any of the brands that the freelancer has worked for. Well-known brands have high expectations and regimented timelines. If the freelancer has worked for them in the past, they can likely adhere to your schedule as well.

▸ **Client references:** If the client history is appealing to you, the next step is to get client references. Sometimes, freelancers work for agencies who have a large brand as their end client. Because the freelancer did work for the large brand, they claim the brand in their client history. It will be important to identify if your candidate is doing this. It's not a deal-breaker, but you should ask to speak with the agency they've worked for as a reference in these cases.

▸ **Freelance history:** Check out the freelancer on LinkedIn and Dribbble at minimum. On LinkedIn, you'll be able to see their job history, recommendations, and connections. On Dribbble, you'll be able to view the content that they are most proud of to get an idea of their preferred aesthetic style. This will help you understand how versatile they are.

▶ **Response to feedback:** Find some projects on their portfolio that are not your favorite and discuss them with your freelancer. Openly critique the work to gauge their response. This serves two purposes. First, it shows the freelancer how you provide feedback. This will help you determine whether they can properly interpret your input. Second, it will help you see how they handle feedback. If they get defensive, then they may not be the best fit for you. If they listen without interruption and provide a respectful response outlining the reasons behind their design choices, you'll get great insight into how they approach design as well as how they manage feedback.

▶ **Their process:** Find some of your favorite projects on your candidate's portfolio. Ask them to walk you through the process of creating those deliverables to better understand their design thinking. Next, ask them how they would approach your work. This will not only help you determine if the freelancer is right for you, but will also help you understand what rate to expect from them.

Key Takeaways It's always good to have a few freelancers in your network that you can trust in a pinch. Sometimes you will need someone to deliver content on a budget while other times you will need to work with someone that can approach your needs with strategy in mind. Because of this, it's best to diversify your team with some lower cost executors and a few higher valued design thinkers. You will still have a large role to play in managing your content needs, but you will also have peace of mind knowing your budget can flex based on the work you are willing and able to shoulder.

CHAPTER 15
BUILDING AN IN-HOUSE TEAM

60% of organizations

cite lack of brand knowledge as a problem when using freelance partnerships and instead opt to build an in-house team, hire an agency, or both

Figure 15.1
Source: Cella Consulting and the BOSS Group, "In-House Creative Industry Report 2019."

For some global companies, such as Coca-Cola and Booking.com, hiring an in-house creative team for regular needs, while partnering with an outside agency for more unique creative requests, often makes the most sense. This is due to the sheer volume of branded content they need to produce, a process that can often be more efficient with a dedicated brand team. If you're trying to decide whether your organization needs to bring creative in-house, or if you want to learn more about life at an agency with an in-house team, this chapter is for you.

THE CHALLENGES OF BUILDING A GREAT TEAM

During Killer's first two years as a company, we tested more than two hundred freelance designers just to find a reliable team of five. While roughly a dozen met our expectations, availability was hard to come by for most. This consistent churn of talent grew impossible to manage and it quickly became clear that the only solution was to build an entirely in-house team.

We had already brought much of our talent in-house, ensuring we had writers and researchers, project managers, and content marketers on staff. This provided dedicated attention for our clients and ensured further success in the work we did. But an in-house team comes with additional costs in the form of salaries, benefits, infrastructure, and more. To manage those costs, we knew we had to grow

our resources slowly, and chose to take our time building an internal team of designers, animators, and developers.

In the process of testing hundreds of freelancers, we found that many designers struggled with visually communicating information and instead relied heavily on text to bring meaning to their design choices. Others could not visualize data appropriately, refused to make requested edits, or took far more time than most to create compelling illustrations. We realized that we were approaching the creation of our design team too broadly in assuming that great portfolios should be the only measure of a great visual communicator.

Such an assumption, we learned, is akin to expecting that anyone who can cook a great meal can also win a Michelin star. This doesn't mean that their craft is any less valuable—it simply means that different experiences require different types of culinary artists. In the same way that chefs specialize in different cuisines and cooking styles, each designer will bring a unique array of skills to the table.

FINDING A TRUE VISUAL COMMUNICATOR

The art of visual communication requires a unique blend of natural capabilities and focused training. Great visual communicators must understand the psychology of speaking visually while also honing their approach to best apply all associated rules. We knew that we could find designers with the necessary talent to deliver great visual communication, but to mold that talent properly and best serve our clients, we needed to provide one-on-one training.

When searching for a great visual communicator, a portfolio can give clues to their natural abilities. Knowing this, we started looking for designers with portfolios that showed a minimum of the following characteristics:

▸ A mastery of typography and page layouts.

▸ At least one project featuring accurate data visualizations.

▸ A portfolio piece outlining their process that at least included a phase for sketching or wireframing prior to starting design.

▸ Illustrations across a wide variety of styles, including character illustrations, full scenes, and iconography.

While this helped to narrow the playing field, we knew that extensive training would still be required to build the right team. We needed to hire designers who would be amenable to this training, have the maturity to manage feedback respectfully, and have the confidence to communicate their design choices to clients. As you consider building an in-house team, a candidate's creative abilities should carry weight, but their values and interpersonal skills must be equally important.

Unlike in the case of a freelancer, the team you bring in-house will work beside you every day. Personality conflicts are few and far between when everyone is remote, but they can easily fester in close quarters.

Because of this, we follow a very strict process when hiring for our in-house team, and never skip the following steps:

▸ **Test attention to detail:** Think back to the rules of visual communication. Almost all of them require attention to key details such as color choices, fonts, small visual cues, and audience expectations. Every role played in the creation of a visual strategy requires an eye for detail to ensure all design choices adhere to the needs of both the organization delivering the content and the audience viewing that content. In addition, most content will require the input of stakeholders. Managing and responding to that detailed feedback can mean the difference between a successful outcome and an utter failure. Find a way to test any candidate's attention to detail up front. This is not an easy skill to teach, so hiring someone that already has this talent honed will be ideal.

▸ **Test problem-solving skills:** Creative content often serves as the solution to a problem. Maybe an organization needs to share an important message with its employees, or maybe a new product offering isn't getting the attention it deserves; whatever the problem may be, it drove the need for visual media. But that's just the first problem that a creative team faces. Over the course of a project, they're sure to encounter myriad problems as they work to put the puzzle pieces of their visual content together. Put candidates through problem-solving exercises to understand how solutions-driven they are before hiring them.

▸ **Test ego and sensitivity:** Creative work is hard. Extremely hard. Designers dedicate dozens of hours to single pieces of content in ways that are emotionally and physically exhausting. When this happens, it can sometimes be hard to hear constructive criticism. To avoid hurting feelings, stakeholders can sometimes sugarcoat feedback, which may help a designer's self-esteem, but will ultimately stand in the way of a successful outcome for the project. Make sure your creative team can lean into criticism, using it as an opportunity to collaborate with stakeholders on solutions, rather than taking the path of least resistance.

▸ **Test values:** Companies that hire and fire by their values see far more success than those that don't. When employees share the same values, they solve interpersonal conflicts by leveraging those same values. However, when values are not a key consideration of the organization, conflicts are more prevalent. It would be a shame to bring on great talent only to lose them after six months. But this is the typical tenure of designers at organizations, in large part because personal conflicts hinder their job satisfaction.

THE COST OF IN-HOUSE

Building an in-house team requires a big investment of time and money, the returns of which can only be realized if the demand for your team's time is consistently high. If you don't have enough work to fill a full-time role, and cannot hire someone part-time, then you're better off hiring a freelancer or working with an agency partner. If, however, you have a predictable influx of content needs, then this investment could save you money in the long term.

When building an in-house team, you must consider the following expenses beyond the cost of a salary or hourly rate:

▸ **Payroll taxes:** While freelancers are 1099 contractors who have to pay their own taxes, an in-house team must be given a W2, which means the employer will be paying a portion of their taxes. Add at least 10 percent to the overall salary to budget for these taxes.

▸ **Benefits:** Check the laws in your state to determine what benefits must be provided to your team. Most states require that employers pay, at minimum, a portion of health care (usually 75 percent), provide paid time off, and allow for paid family and medical leave.

▸ **Infrastructure:** While your "in-house" team might be a group of employees all working remotely, it's far more likely that they'll be working from your office. This means you'll need to invest in desks, chairs, whiteboards, tablets, computers, utilities, among other expenses. Be prepared to take on those costs and expect them to grow as your team grows.

▸ **Software:** To create great visual content, you'll need the Adobe Creative Cloud at minimum. This comes at a monthly cost that can be negotiated based on team size. Other great software and services to consider are outlined in Appendix B of this book.

▸ **Unemployment insurance:** Some states require a percentage be paid per employee paycheck to cover unemployment benefits. Others require that you find a private provider for this insurance. In either situation, you will need to pay into unemployment for each person you hire.

▸ **Employment practices liability (EPL) insurance:** While businesses require many different insurance policies, EPL insurance rates are directly correlated with the number of people an organization employs. So as you grow your team, you must consider how that could impact your rate. If you're doing work on behalf of clients outside your organization, you'll need solid insurance to protect your company in the case of a lawsuit as well as to protect your clients. If you're only doing internal work, your insurance needs are probably already taken care of by your employer.

▸ **State and city taxes:** Tax law varies throughout the country, but some cities and states include a head tax, which is typically a flat rate charged per employee per year.

These examples assume you are hiring in the United States. If you're hiring elsewhere, it's likely these won't all apply to you, but additional costs based on your location may apply. And regardless of where you live, you'll need to pay your team a predictable wage, whether hourly or salaried. Set your pay rate based on the cost of living in your location.

When building an in-house team of creatives, you should try to establish competitive salaries so you can attract the best talent. Check sites like Salary.com and GlassDoor.com to get an idea of typical pay rates in your city or region.

In addition to finding a team that fits your needs, you'll need to ensure your processes and communication style fit their needs. Creative teams that work in-house for a single brand or family of brands can often feel taken advantage of, or can grow indifferent if they're not consistently challenged. As a result, they often find themselves jumping from company to company to continue their own professional development. You will need to regularly hone your process to avoid these issues, which are among the top reported challenges that in-house creative teams face today (Figure 15.2).

What are the leading challenges US in-house creative teams face in 2019?

0   1   2   3   4   5   6   7

Speed at which creative teams are expected to work

5.44

Volume of demand for creative work

5.35

Being a strategic contributor to meeting organizational goals

4.36

Communicating with clients and meeting expectations

3.86

Increasing variety of marketing channels that need creative

3.79

New technologies that change the way teams work

2.79

Retaining and supporting creative staff

2.42

Scale 1–7

1 = Least challenging

7 = Most challenging

Figure 15.2
Source: InSource and inMotionNow, "2019 In-House Creative Management Report."

Key Takeaways If you're looking to deliver a wide variety of visual content on a regular basis, an in-house team can fortify your organization and lay the foundation for long-term success. The right in-house team ensures reliable talent, consistent quality, and a personalized approach that is hard to find if you're relying on freelancers alone. Building an in-house team may not be for everyone, but the benefits will outweigh the investment if your content needs are substantial.

POST-SCRIPT

| *"What's past is prologue."*

—*William Shakespeare*
The Tempest

I am writing these words on the final day of 2019. Tomorrow, a new decade will begin, one that will bring new ideas, innovation, and adventure not yet imagined. At the dawn of 2010, I could not have predicted the decade that was in store for me, just as I cannot predict what is to come over the next ten years.

In 2010, I was an SEO manager at a company called All Star Directories in Seattle, Washington. I had a passion for visual storytelling, but I never expected to make a career out of it. I identified only as a marketer. The concept of being a creative or a visual strategist seemed foreign to me. I knew I wanted to venture out on my own, but had a very clear—and very different— vision of what that experience would look like.

When I left the company in June of that year, All Star's CEO, Doug Brown, asked if he could show me something. He walked me through the office, over to an infographic poster in the tech department. The poster, which had been released in 2009, was called "The Puget Sound Tech Universe."

The design depicted the myriad ways in which tech companies in Seattle were linked. All Star, whose founder had come from Microsoft, had its own place on the map, linked to the Microsoft hub. Doug pointed to the All Star label, and from it drew an imaginary line with his finger to an empty place on the map. "One day, your company will go right here," he told me.

His words of encouragement fueled me. When I had been faced with a competing and financially better job offer, Doug was the reason I came to work for All Star instead. He was a charismatic leader who always brought optimism into the office. He inspired people around his vision and wasn't afraid to roll up his sleeves to do the work himself when needed. I knew that if I could even harness one iota of his leadership skills, I could find success.

In the decade since, my entire world has changed. Together with my team, I have built a multimillion-dollar agency that has made the Inc. 5000 list four years in a row. I've spoken at more than 175 conferences around the world, and I'm considered a thought leader in the realm of visual strategy; I've also become an Inc.com columnist and a LinkedIn Learning instructor. My years are planned before they even start, with nearly 80 percent of my time dedicated to travel to see clients, speak, and run educational workshops. And that tech universe poster? Not only is Killer on it—we were hired to design the updated version in 2015 (Figure 12.1)!

Through all of the forward momentum, we've also seen immense transitions. My spouse changed careers to travel with me, my cofounder and I parted ways, and my executive team became both friends and partners in our journey. Our offerings evolved year after year, leading us to change our company name. And at the beginning of 2019, Killer became part of the LRW Group of companies under the helm of Kelton Global. This exciting relationship has just begun, with plenty of new opportunities to explore as we leverage our family of companies to better serve our clients.

I have been lucky to surround myself with a team of immense talent, empathy, and grit. United by our passion for creating high-quality visual media in combination with a sense of duty to always do what's right, I have found my tribe in my team. We have all learned a great deal from each other, have made what seemed like insurmountable mistakes, and have come out the other side all the better for it.

Today, after a decade immersed in visual content, I have turned to text to share everything that I've learned. This, my first book, incorporates ten years of lessons forged from a little bit of trial and error and a lot of listening: embracing harsh criticism with an open mind and treating positive feedback as a guidepost.

As William Shakespeare wrote, "What's past is prologue." In this book, I've shared my past to help inform your future. Now that you've reached the end, you should have a great deal more context to inspire your next steps. I hope the lessons in this book have empowered you. These are the lessons I have had to learn on my journey to becoming a visual strategist, and I hope that you, too, can take what you've learned and proudly say: I am not a graphic designer. I am a visual strategist.

APPENDIX A: TERMS AND DEFINITIONS

While countless terms and phrases are used regularly in the visual communication industry, I chose to include only a select few here. I consider these the most common and important lingo to know. If you're not a designer, the terminology that follows will help you better communicate with designers. If you are a designer, the definitions will help you better present your ideas and your work to stakeholders.

VISUAL COMMUNICATION

Visual communication graphically represents information to efficiently and effectively create meaning. When necessary, limited text is used to explicate that meaning. There are two distinct products of visual communication: information visualization and visual storytelling.

INFORMATION VISUALIZATION

Information visualization aims to convey meaning from information as quickly as possible. The primary focus is to educate the viewer, not persuade them to form a specific opinion.

VISUAL STORYTELLING

Visual storytelling uses visual communication to craft a narrative. It can be used across all visual media, including infographics, motion graphics, and interactive content. Education is one of the end goals, but this approach aims to persuade the viewer to reach a specific conclusion.

VISUAL IDENTITY

A visual identity is a codified system of visual elements that express a brand's purpose, values, ambitions, characteristics, and promise. It translates a brand's identity into an easily identifiable style, and is typically housed in a brand book or set of brand guidelines. A well-developed visual identity will so accurately capture a brand's story that a casual observer should be able to view any piece of brand collateral and immediately understand the brand's fundamental character.

VISUAL LANGUAGE

A visual language is a tactical deployment of a brand's visual identity, created for a specific campaign, initiative, product, or audience in order to achieve specific communication and business goals. A visual language draws on select components of the brand's visual identity, as well as introducing new visual elements (such as character- and icon-illustration styles, data-visualization styles, and more), in order to create a unique aesthetic deployment of the brand. It is a "style guide" for a campaign.

While a brand's visual identity is necessarily broad (as it attempts to anticipate all possible visual deployments of the brand), a visual language is more focused and specialized in order to provide tactical guidance for the specific deliverables comprising a given campaign. A visual language can't always answer the question, "Is 'X' on-brand?"

VISUAL STRATEGY

Visual strategy encompasses the creative and analytic decisions that inform any visual expression of a brand. That expression could be a visual identity or a visual language. It could also direct a visual content marketing initiative by strategizing on what content to produce, what it should look like, and where it should live both online and offline.

The visual strategy you develop for a particular engagement should define what you are going to produce, how you are going to produce it (i.e., the creative direction), and where it should be deployed (including how elements should link to one another). All of those decisions are made after thorough consideration of the primary stakeholder's brand, audience, and communication goals.

VISUAL COMMUNICATION CAMPAIGN

A visual communication campaign targets one or more common goals using strategic visual content. It is a series of branded media that lives within a defined art direction (i.e., a visual language) and typically does not require external explanation to give context, relying instead on visual content to drive meaning. Campaigns may include graphic design, animation, interactivity, and more to aid in the delivery of the main message.

Definitions written by Josh Miles, president and chief creative officer at Killer Visual Strategies.

APPENDIX B: TOOLS

There is an abundance of tools available to visual strategists, but some are more useful than others. I've listed only my favorite tools in this appendix, alongside explanations of why we use them at my company, Killer Visual Strategies.

THE ADOBE CREATIVE CLOUD

In Adobe's own words, "Creative Cloud is a collection of 20+ desktop and mobile apps and services for photography, design, video, web, UX, and more. You can take your ideas to new places with Photoshop on the iPad, draw and paint with Fresco, and design for 3D and AR."

The Adobe Creative Cloud is the go-to solution for all designers and creatives looking to develop custom visual content. As I write this book, individual apps cost $20.99 per month, but you can access every available Adobe product for $52.99 per month. The most popular tools used by visual communicators include:

▸ **Adobe Illustrator:** Approximately 90 percent of the projects we create at Killer Visual Strategies start in Adobe Illustrator, and at least half of them only require Illustrator to produce.

▸ **Adobe After Effects:** To create great motion graphics, you need a great animation tool. After Effects is that tool.

▸ **Adobe InDesign:** While InDesign has many applications, we choose to use it when creating multipage, print-ready content.

▸ **Adobe Premiere Pro:** For any live-action video editing, color correcting, and more, Adobe Premiere is the answer.

▸ **Adobe Dreamweaver:** Many seasoned developers choose to code outside of Dreamweaver, but for those who are just getting started or who love a WYSIWYG editor, Dreamweaver provides ample tools to code the website of ... well, your dreams.

▸ **Adobe Photoshop:** While some choose to create the bulk of their designs in Photoshop, we've learned that, for some applications, it can be arduous to do so. Instead, we use Photoshop for adding textures and effects to illustrations and, of course, for touching up photos.

▸ **Adobe Fonts:** A world of font options is at your fingertips with Adobe Fonts (formerly called Typekit). Not only can you add new and unique fonts to your Adobe apps, but you can also find fonts that browsers will properly display. In other words, you can make your interactive content carry forward the rule of WTF as well.

▸ **Adobe XD:** When wireframing interactive content or prototyping design, Adobe XD provides a streamlined process.

▸ **Adobe Dimension:** As 3D design becomes more popular, Adobe Dimension will continue to evolve into a go-to tool. Right now, though, it has a lot of great 3D applications to compete with, including Cinema 4D and Clay.

These tools can be used independently of one another or in tandem with each other. For example, a typical motion graphic can require using Adobe Illustrator, Photoshop, After Effects, and Premiere Pro to create a great end product. When my creative director designed this book, he used a combination of Adobe Illustrator and InDesign.

LINKEDIN LEARNING AND LYNDA.COM

Lynda.com and LinkedIn Learning offer perhaps the best online learning experience for graphic design, content strategy, and related skills. In 2015, LinkedIn purchased Lynda.com to bring their courses to a far wider audience. Since it's possible that the Lynda brand will eventually disappear in favor of making LinkedIn Learning the only destination for their content, I'll refer to them as LinkedIn Learning going forward.

Unlike most online learning platforms, LinkedIn Learning differentiated itself early on by carefully curating its instructors. Instead of just anyone being able to upload a course, LinkedIn Learning instructors have always had to be invited into the fold. They spend months writing their course scripts with a skilled producer at their side to ensure that all key points are covered. Once scripting is done, they are invited to LinkedIn Learning's professional recording studios to ensure a high-quality end deliverable.

In their own words—which speak for LinkedIn Learning, as well:

Lynda.com is a leading online learning platform that helps anyone learn business, software, technology, and creative skills to achieve personal and professional goals. Through individual, corporate, academic, and government subscriptions, members have access to the Lynda.com video library of engaging, top-quality courses taught by recognized industry experts. For 20 years, Lynda.com has helped students, leaders, IT and design pros, project managers— anyone in any role—develop software, creative, and business skills. Now part of LinkedIn, Lynda.com serves more than 10,000 organizations. With tutorials in five languages, Lynda.com is a global platform for success.

To learn more about visual strategy and visual communication, check out my courses on LinkedIn Learning including:

▸ Good Design Drives Business

▸ Visual Communication for Business

▸ Developing Visual Campaigns

▸ Learning Infographic Design

THE NOUN PROJECT

As I mentioned in rule 2 (small visual cues have a large impact), Noun Project is an amazing resource for any visual communicator. I reached out to Sofya Polyakov, the CEO and cofounder of Noun Project, and asked if she could share some thoughts about her service for this book. Here is what she told me:

At Noun Project, we believe visual language has the power to shape, reinforce, and change our perceptions of the world. Since 2011 our community of creatives from around the world has been building the most diverse and extensive collection of iconography ever created. The Noun Project collection represents topics as broad as design and technology, pop culture, nostalgia, nature, architecture, space, and artificial intelligence.

As a leader in visual communication, Noun Project has a responsibility to not only provide our users with existing iconography, but also create a new visual language for concepts yet to be defined. This conviction has led us to host Iconathons—design workshops that engage the general public in building the world's visual language by creating mission-driven iconography

that is contributed to the public domain, free for all to use.

Symbols are some of the best universal tools to overcome language and cultural communication barriers, and it's more important than ever that they communicate in a socially conscious way. To create more representation and inclusion in iconography, Noun Project has spearheaded initiatives like the "Redefining Women Icon Collection," featuring over 60 public domain icons of women in leadership positions; writing guidelines for depicting race in iconography; and strict curatorial rules.

LOST TYPE

If you're looking for trending fonts, look no further than Lost Type. Unlike in the case of other font banks online, you won't find yourself overwhelmed by too many options at Lost Type. Instead, you'll find a handful of carefully curated and stunning font options to choose from. Lost Type is a co-op of artists, so make sure you give a donation with each font that you download.

In their own words:

Lost Type is a Collaborative Digital Type Foundry. Operated and managed by Riley Cran (and originally cofounded with Tyler Galpin), Lost Type is the first of its kind, a Pay-What-You-Want type foundry. Since 2011 Lost Type has been a source for unique typefaces, with a collection of over 50 different faces from contributors all over the world. 100% of the funds from sales of these fonts go directly to their respective designers. Lost Type fonts have been used across the world, and recently have been featured in projects for Nike, Starbucks, Disney, and the president of the United States. Lost Type continues to be dedicated to the idea that quality fonts should be made available to anyone who wants to create an individual piece of characterful design.

DRIBBBLE

Part social network, part job board, part art gallery, Dribbble is for designers and organizations looking to find great designers. Dribbble is a place where designers can share their work, get feedback from creatives they admire, and check out the job board for freelance opportunities. Businesses, meanwhile, can find amazing talent by viewing thousands of portfolios while using Dribbble's unique filter functions to narrow their search.

At Killer, Dribbble is the first place we go to find great local talent when it's time to hire another designer. As a visual communication agency, we also have our own Dribbble page, where our design team can post their work and receive candid feedback from the community. It helps us hone our craft, share what inspires us, and get inspired by a global community of artists.

In their own words:

Tens of millions of people look for design inspiration and feedback on Dribbble. We help players like you share small screenshots ("shots") to show off your current projects, boost your portfolio, and love what you do—no matter what kind of creative professional you are.

Founded in 2009, we are a bootstrapped and profitable company helping design talent share, grow, and get hired by over 40,000 of today's most innovative brands around the world.

COLOURLOVERS

When looking for a great color palette, there are two websites our team loves to frequent. One is the aforementioned Dribbble (where you can see color palettes in action) and the other is COLOURLovers. On this site, designers can search for color palettes based on any keyword they can imagine. For instance, if they're looking to represent a particular mood, all they have to do is type that mood ("happy," "sad," etc.) into the search bar and see what appears.

Colors within each palette are presented in different ratios to suggest which color should be your primary, secondary, and so on. When you find a color you like, simply click it to reveal hex and RGB values. You can also use the "create" tool to test your own color palettes.

In their own words:

> COLOURlovers is an international creative community that helps people discover their inner designer. We provide people with a wealth of user created and shared color inspiration as well as tools that make the creative process as simple as possible. Whether you're simply looking for a color palette to kickstart your next project or want to produce a piece of vector art, we have the tools and services to help anybody go from design inspiration to execution.

APPENDIX C: PRODUCTION TIME ESTIMATES

Great visual content takes time, but if you aren't a designer, you might not realize just how much time must be invested into custom work. There are countless low-cost providers that rely heavily on cheap labor, templates, stock imagery, or a combination of all three to maintain their rates. With providers like these, you may like the price point, but when you're paying for a cookie-cutter solution, you'll get cookie-cutter results. In other words, it can become extremely hard to ensure your brand shines through, your target audience is accommodated, and your goals are truly considered.

To help you understand what you should pay for high-quality visual content, the table below outlines the hours required to create something customized for your brand, audiences, and project goals.

The hour estimates in this table represent the level of effort required to create a custom, high-quality end deliverable that adheres to the rules of visual communication. These are the total combined hours required of a full project team, including at minimum a project manager, content writer and strategist, and designer. In the case of animated or interactive content, an animator, editor, developer, and/or sound designer's time is also included.

Finally, it's important to note that these hour estimates are based on averages only. A request for more illustration than normal may increase hours. A request for shortened content may decrease hours. Use these estimates as a jumping-off point, and collaborate on solutions if unique needs lead to an unmanageable scope.

Type of Media	Total Project Team Hours
Infographics	25–35 hours
One-sheeters (single- and double-sided) and trifold brochures	20–45 hours
E-books (per 10 pages)	55–80 hours
Short-form animated videos and GIFs up to 15 seconds long	15–20 hours
Motion graphics up to 90 seconds long, entry-level (no character animation; everything animates in x and y space only)	80–110 hours
Motion graphics up to 90 seconds long, mid-level (no character animation; items can animate in x, y, and z space; full sound design and original score)	110–130 hours
Motion graphics up to 90 seconds long, expert level (character animation; complex transitions; animation on a 3D field; full sound design and original score)	150–200 hours
Interactive content, small widgets	40–80 hours
Interactive content, parallax landing page (note that length and on-screen animation both greatly impact time)	100–250 hours

APPENDIX D: A TIMELINE OF VISUAL COMMUNICATION

One week after I completed the first draft of this timeline, the discovery of a new cave painting was announced—a painting that was five thousand years older than what had been established for decades as the earliest-known piece of cave art. While we were able to adjust the content to represent this new finding (which kicks off the timeline), it was an exciting reminder of the fact that we are still discovering the world around us.

The snapshot of the past that this timeline represents can change, but I've tried to deliver a useful overview of how visual communication has evolved since its earliest appearances in human history. Understanding the history of visual communication can help you plan your own future as a visual strategist.

All sources are cited in the Resources section of this book.

THE FIRST VISUAL STORYTELLING

A hunting scene painted on the walls of a cave in Sulawesi, Indonesia, represents the oldest known example of visual storytelling in human history.

EUROPE'S EARLIEST CAVE PAINTING

A red disk in Spain's el Castillo cave comprises Europe's oldest known cave painting.

THE OLDEST LAND MAP

The first known map of land is drawn on a mammoth's tusk in what is today the Czech Republic.

GROWING DETAIL & VARIETY IN CAVE PAINTINGS

The Lascaux caves in France contain nearly two thousand unique abstract, human, and animal figures, including:

364 horses
90 stags
1 17-foot-long bull

41,900 BCE

38,800 BCE

ca. 25,000 BCE

ca. 18,000 BCE

THE FIRST ASTRONOMICAL MAP

The oldest-known map of the night sky is drawn on the walls of the Lascaux caves.

EARLY VISUAL STORYTELLING

Drawings and hieroglyphics combine to tell a story in the Egyptian Book of the Dead.

VASES THAT TELL A STORY

Vases that show black silhouettes on an orange clay background—a style developed in Corinth—tell foundational stories in Greek mythology.

THE FIRST PAPER

Paper is invented by Ts'ai Lun, a member of the Han Dynasty emperor's court.

ca. 14,000 BCE

ca. 1275 BCE

700 BCE

ca. 105 CE

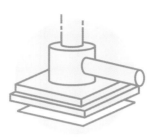

ILLUMINATED MANUSCRIPTS

Western Europe sees its first illuminated manuscripts, which combine illustrations with stylized text.

THE FIRST STAR ATLAS

The Dunhuang Star Atlas is the earliest known astronomical atlas manuscript.

THE ARRIVAL OF MOVABLE TYPE

Chinese artisan Bi Sheng invents movable type.

THE GUTENBERG PRESS

Johannes Gutenberg engineers the first printing press in Europe.

500

ca. 700

ca. 1041–48

1450

THE FIRST MODERN ATLAS

Teatrum Orbis Terrarum, the world's first modern atlas, is published.

THE VISUAL TIMELINE IS BORN

Jacques Barbeu-Dubourg creates the first visual annotated timeline of history.

THE FIRST PUBLISHED INFOGRAPHICS

William Playfair publishes *The Commercial and Political Atlas,* where he premieres the first-ever bar and line graphs. This book therefore comprises the first data visualization–powered infographics in print. Playfair will later invent the area chart and the pie chart.

THE REPRODUCTION OF VISUAL ART

Alois Senefelder invents lithography, which enables the mass production of not just text, but also visual art.

1570   **1753**   **1786**   **1798**

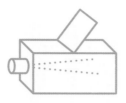

**PHOTOGRAPHY
EMERGES**

Joseph Nicéphore
Niépce takes
the world's first
photograph of a real-
world scene.

**DATA-POWERED
SOCIAL SCIENCE**

André-Michel Guerry,
a French lawyer, is
among the first to
use different levels of
shading to visualize
data. He maps data
related to illiteracy,
crime, and other
social issues.

**USING DATA
VISUALIZATION TO
TRACK DISEASE**

A map created by
John Snow, a British
physician, traces the
source of a cholera
epidemic in London
back to a single
water pump. When
the pump is closed,
infections numbers
go down. This data
visualization and the
subsequent cholera
abatement will later
serve as proof that
contact with bacteria
spreads disease.

**DATA VISUALIZATION
AND PUBLIC POLICY**

Florence Nightingale
publishes a polar area
diagram (her own
invention) proving
that most deaths in
the Crimean War were
caused by disease, not
fighting. It becomes
one of the earliest
data visualizations
to influence public
policy.

1827

1830s

1854

1858

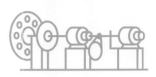

EARLY COLOR PHOTOGRAPHY

The first-ever color photograph is produced by James C. Maxwell, a Scottish physicist.

THE FIRST FILM

The world's first motion picture—a film of a running horse—is recorded by Eadweard Muybridge. The movie is intended to resolve a dispute about whether all four hooves of a running horse ever leave the ground simultaneously.

THE MECHANICAL TELEVISION

Paul Gottlieb Nipkow, a German engineer, pioneers a rotating disk that powers mechanical televisions— precursors to electric TVs.

THE LONDON TUBE MAP

Harry Beck's stylized diagram of the London Underground Tube emphasized clarity of information over accurate portrayal of the lines, revolutionizing information design.

1861   **1877**   **1884**   **1933**

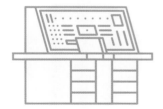

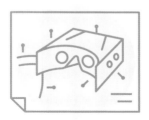

THE ARRIVAL OF VIDEO GAMES

"Cathode Ray Tube Amusement Device," a single-player video game, emerges as one of the earliest examples of interactive visual storytelling.

COMMERCIAL COMPUTING

The Ferranti Mark I emerges as the world's first commercially sold computer. The UNIVAC 1, premiering the same year, attracts more widespread public attention.

A PIONEER OF AUGMENTED REALITY

Cinematographer Morton Heilig premieres the world's first augmented reality device, called Sensorama.

A PRECURSOR TO VIRTUAL REALITY HEADSETS

Heilig patents the Telesphere Mask, the world's earliest head-mounted display.

1947　　**1951**　　**1957**　　**1960**

THE HOME VIDEO GAME ········· **THE CONTEMPORARY PICTOGRAM**
SYSTEM

The Magnavox Odyssey
emerges as the first-ever home
video game console. The Atari,
which will ultimately be much
more successful, arrives on the
market just a few
months later.

Designer Otl Aicher's pictograms,
designed for the 1972 Summer
Olympics in Munich, revolutionize the
use of clear iconography for universal
communication. Most famous among
his designs were the near-ubiquitous
male and female restroom signs.

A VR INTERFACE

Videoplace becomes
the earliest virtual
reality interface.

A LEADER IN DATA VIZ

With the publication of
his first book, *The Visual
Display of Quantitative
Information,* Edward
Tufte emerges as the
world's leading theorist
in data visualization,
graphic design, and
statistics.

**THE PRIVATIZATION
OF THE INTERNET**

The US government
begins to permit the
privatization of the
internet, which marks
the foundations of
the web as we know it
today.

1972   **1975**   **1983**   **1994**

CONTENT IS KING

Bill Gates published his now-famous essay, "Content Is King," predicting how content creation—including the dissemination of visual content such as games and video— would drive the future of the internet.

THE INVENTION OF THE EMOJI

Japanese artist Shigetaka Kurita designs the world's first 176 emojis for a Japanese mobile internet platform.

FACEBOOK LAUNCHES

With Facebook's emergence, an entirely new way of sharing visual stories and content is born. Two years later, the platform will be open to everyone aged thirteen or older.

2007: THE FIRST SMARTPHONE

Apple launches its first iPhone, kicking off a new era of mobile-first content creation.

1996   **1999**   **2004**   **2007**

THE ARRIVAL OF INSTAGRAM

Instagram makes visual content more central to its platform than any of its predecessors. Within a year of launch, five hundred thousand people per week are signing up.

PINTEREST DOMINATES

Visual content–centered site Pinterest drives more business traffic to sites than Google+, YouTube, and LinkedIn combined.

OCULUS DRIVES THE FUTURE OF VR

Oculus, a VR headset company, launches a Kickstarter campaign that will raise $2.5 million. Two years later, Facebook will acquire Oculus for $2 billion.

VISUAL CONTENT & BREAKING NEWS

25% of all tweets about Hurricane Sandy included photos and videos, making visual media fundamental to the dissemination of timely information.

VISUAL CONTENT DOMINATES MEDIA CHANNELS

The *New York Times*'s most popular story of the year is an infographic and interactive questionnaire that visualizes US regional accents.

ADVENTURES IN AR

Google announces Google Glass, its augmented reality beta project.

2010   **2012**   **2013**

SOCIAL-MEDIA USE AT AN ALL TIME HIGH

82% of US adults aged 18–49 are on social media.

THE DOMINANCE OF VIDEO

Cisco projects that **82%** of all internet traffic will be video by 2022.

2018

2019

RESOURCES

Adobe. "The State of Content: Expectations on the Rise." October 2015. https://blogs.adobe.com/creative/files/2015/12/Adobe-State-of-Content-Report.pdf.

Adobe and Econsultancy. "Digital Intelligence Briefing: 2018 Digital Trends." 2018. https://www.adobe.com/content/dam/acom/en/modal-offers/pdfs/0060629.en.aec.whitepaper.econsultancy-2018-digital-trends-US.pdf.

Amos, Jonathan. "Red Dot Becomes 'Oldest Cave Art.'" BBC News, June 15, 2012. https://www.bbc.com/news/science-environment-18449711.

Aronica, Janet. "Pinterest Drives More Referral Traffic Than Google Plus, YouTube and LinkedIn Combined." *Shareaholic*, January 31, 2012. https://www.shareaholic.com/blog/pinterest-referral-traffic.

Associated Press. "Number of Active Users at Facebook over the Years." *Yahoo Finance*, October 23, 2012. https://finance.yahoo.com/news/number-active-users-facebook-over-years-214600186--finance.html.

Bino, Eyal. "The Gig Economy May Be Booming but Freelancers Are Still Bad with Money." *Forbes*, March 14, 2019. https://www.forbes.com/sites/eyalbino/2019/03/14/the-future-of-work-is-bad-with-money-tech-startups-can-change-that/#165279133492.

Biography.com Editors. "James C. Maxwell Biography." Biography.com, June 23, 2019. https://www.biography.com/scientist/james-c-maxwell#synopsis.

Blanchfield, Anthony, James Hardy, and Samuele Marcora. "Non-Conscious Visual Cues Related to Affect and Action Alter Perception of Effort and Endurance Performance." *Frontiers in Human Neuroscience* (December 11, 2014). https://doi.org/10.3389/fnhum.2014.00967.

Bottomley, Paul A., and John R. Doyle. "The Interactive Effects of Colors and Products on Perceptions of Brand Logo Appropriateness." *Marketing Theory* 6, no. 1 (March 1, 2006): 63–83. https://doi.org/10.1177/1470593106061263.

Bower, Bruce. "A Nearly 44,000-Year-Old Hunting Scene Is the Oldest Known Storytelling Art." *Science News*, December 11, 2019. https://www.sciencenews.org/article/nearly-44000-year-old-hunting-scene-is-oldest-storytelling-art.

British Library. "Chinese Star Chart." Accessed January 28, 2020. https://www.bl.uk/collection-items/chinese-star-chart.

Brown, Abram. "Kevin Systrom in His Own Words: How Instagram Was Founded and Became the World's Favorite
        Social Media App." *Forbes*, September 25, 2018. https://www.forbes.com/sites/abrambrown/2018/09/25/
        kevin-systrom-in-his-own-words-how--instagram-was-founded-and-became-the-worlds-favorite-social-media-
        app/#7ab21ca142bf.

Brysbaert, Marc. "How Many Words Do We Read Per Minute? A Review and Meta-analysis of Reading Rate." *PsyArXiv*
        (December 10, 2019). https://psyarxiv.com/xynwg.

Callaham, Sheila. "Are You a Baby Boomer Looking for Work? Where to Find the Best Opportunities." *Forbes*, March 21,
        2019. https://www.forbes.com/sites/sheilacallaham/2019/03/21/are-you-a-baby-boomer-looking-for-work-
        where-to-find-the-best-opportunities/#6fbc0e9360bd.

Carlson, Nicholas. "At Last—the Full Story of How Facebook Was Founded." *Business Insider*, March 5, 2010. https://
        www.businessinsider.com/how-facebook-was-founded-2010-3.

Carmody, Dennis P., and Michael Lewis. "Brain Activation When Hearing One's Own and Others' Names." *Brain Research*
        1116, no. 1 (October 20, 2006): 153–158. https://doi.org/10.1016/j.brainres.2006.07.121.

Caumont, Andrea. "12 Trends Shaping Digital News." Pew Research Center, October 16, 2013. https://www.pewresearch.
        org/fact-tank/2013/10/16/12-trends-shaping-digital-news.

Cella Consulting and the BOSS Group. "In-House Creative Industry Report 2019." 2019. https://cella-live-
        54c7dc51ec5141f1b6f5f312fd4-5b9175f.aldryn-media.com/filer_public/b0/81/b081bc0d-8c3f-428f-9e6f-
        38c62852434e/2019_ihcsir_report_by_boss_and_cella.pdf.

Cisco. "Cisco Visual Networking Index: Forecast and Trends, 2017–2022 White Paper." February 27, 2019. https://www.
        cisco.com/c/en/us/solutions/collateral/service-provider/visual-networking-index-vni/white-paper-c11-741490.
        html.

Clark, Andrew J., Maya Elston, and Mary Louise Hart. "An Overview of Athenian Painted Ceramic Vases." Khan Academy,
        accessed January 28, 2020. https://www.khanacademy.org/partner-content/getty-museum/antiquities/getty-
        ancient-greek-vases/a/an-overview-of-athenian-painted-ceramic-vases.

Clark, Ruth C., and Richard E. Mayer. *e-Learning and the Science of Instruction: Proven Guidelines for Consumers and Designers of Multimedia Learning.* Hoboken: John Wiley & Sons, Inc., 2016.

Click Laboratory. "Numara Software Case Study." Accessed January 20, 2020. https://www.clicklaboratory.com/case-studies/increasing-sales-pipeline-with-adaptive-web-design.

Computer History Museum. "Timeline of Computer History." Accessed January 28, 2020. https://www.computerhistory.org/timeline.

Congdon, Luis. "Why What Bill Gates Said about the Internet in 1996 Is Truer Than Ever Today." *Entrepreneur*, December 5, 2017. https://www.entrepreneur.com/article/305300.

Coye, Noël, and the Bradshaw Foundation. "The Cave Paintings of the Lascaux Cave." Bradshaw Foundation, accessed January 28, 2020. http://www.bradshawfoundation.com/lascaux.

Dean, Tomer. "User Generated Content vs Stock Photos." Bllush, October 18, 2016. https://www.bllush.com/battle-conversion-rates-user-generated-content-vs-stock-photos-data.

Deloitte. "Digital Media Trends Survey, 13th Edition." Accessed January 24, 2020. https://www2.deloitte.com/us/en/insights/industry/technology/digital-media-trends-consumption-habits-survey.html.

Demand Gen Report. "2015 Content Preferences Survey." 2015. https://www.demandgenreport.com/resources/research/2015-content-preferences-survey-buyers-value-content-packages-interactive-content.

Dijksterhuis, Ap., Pamela K. Smith, Rick B. van Baaren, and Daniël H. J. Wigboldus. "The Unconscious Consumer: Effects of Environment on Consumer Behavior." *Journal of Consumer Psychology* 15, no. 3 (2005): 193–202. https://doi.org/10.1207/s15327663jcp1503_3.

Edelman. "2019 Edelman Trust Barometer." Daniel J. Edelman Holdings, Inc., April 5, 2019. https://www.edelman.amsterdam/news-awards/2019-edelman-trust-barometer.

———. "2019 Edelman Trust Barometer Special Report: In Brands We Trust?" Daniel J. Edelman Holdings, Inc., June 18, 2019. https://www.edelman.com/research/trust-barometer-special-report-in-brands-we-trust.

Editors of Encyclopædia Britannica. "Lithography." *Encyclopædia Britannica*, accessed January 28, 2020. https://www.
     britannica.com/technology/lithography.

———. "Paul Gottlieb Nipkow." *Encyclopædia Britannica*, accessed January 28, 2020. https://www.britannica.com/
     biography/Paul-Gottlieb-Nipkow.

Friendly, Michael, and Daniel J. Denis. "Milestones in the History of Thematic Cartography, Statistical Graphics, and Data
     Visualization." Accessed January 28, 2020. http://datavis.ca/milestones/index.php?group=1700s&mid=ms80.

Gates, Bill. "Content Is King." Microsoft. January 3, 1996. http://web.archive.org/web/20010126005200/http://www.
     microsoft.com/billgates/columns/1996essay/essay960103.asp.

Gilbert, Ben. "It's Been over 12 Years since the iPhone Debuted—Look How Primitive the First One Seems Today."
     Business Insider, July 22, 2019. https://www.businessinsider.com/first-phone-anniversary-2016-12.

Grady, Denise. "The Vision Thing: Mainly in the Brain." *Discover*, May 31, 1993. https://www.discovermagazine.com/
     mind/the-vision-thing-mainly-in-the-brain.

Gregg, Dawn G., and Steven Walczak. "The Relationship between Website Quality, Trust and Price Premiums at Online
     Auctions." *Electronic Commerce Research* 10 (2010): 1–25. https://doi.org/10.1007/s10660-010-9044-2.

Handley, Lucy. "Firms Are Taking More Marketing Functions In-House. Here's Why." CNBC, March 4, 2019. https://www.
     cnbc.com/2019/03/04/firms-are-taking-more-marketing-functions-in-house-heres-why.html.

Harley, Robin. "James Vicary: Experiment & Overview." Study.com, accessed January 16, 2020. https://study.com/
     academy/lesson/james-vicary-experiment-lesson-quiz.html.

Harris, Beth, and Steven Zucker. "Last Judgement of Hunefer, from His Tomb." Khan Academy, accessed January 28,
     2020. Video. https://www.khanacademy.org/humanities/ap-art-history/ancient-mediterranean-ap/ancient-
     egypt-ap/v/judgement-in-the-presence-of-osiris-hunefer-s-book-of-the-dead.

History.com Editors. "Printing Press." HISTORY, October 10, 2019. https://www.history.com/topics/inventions/
     printing-press.

History.com Editors. "Printing Press." HISTORY, October 10, 2019. https://www.history.com/topics/inventions/
     printing-press.

Hitlin, Paul. "Internet, Social Media Use and Device Ownership in U.S. Have Plateaued after Years of Growth." Pew
     Research Center, September 28, 2018. https://www.pewresearch.org/fact-tank/2018/09/28/internet-social-
     media-use-and-device-ownership-in-u-s-have-plateaued-after-years-of-growth.

In-House Agency Forum and Forrester Research. "In-House Agencies Today: 2018 State-of-the-Industry Report." 2018.
     https://www.ihaforum.org/in-house-agencies-today.

INQUIRER. "Search Results: The Everywhere Girl." Incisive Business Media Limited, accessed January 20, 2020. https://
     www.theinquirer.net/search?page=2&query=the+everywhere+girl&sort=relevance.

InSource and inMotionNow. "2019 In-House Creative Management Report." inMotionNow, Inc., 2019. https://www.
     inmotionnow.com/project-workflow/in-house-creative-management-report-2019.

Interaction Design Foundation. "Augmented Reality—The Past, the Present, and the Future." 2019. https://www.
     interaction-design.org/literature/article/augmented-reality-the-past-the-present-and-the-future.

Jain, Rachna. "7 Ways to Use Psychological Influence with Social Media Content." Social Media Examiner, May 10, 2010.
     https://www.socialmediaexaminer.com/7-ways-to-use-psychological-influence-with-social-media-content.

Jensen, Eric. Brain-Based Learning: The New Paradigm of Teaching. Thousand Oaks, CA: Corwin Press, 2008.

Kang, Mihyun, and Sejung Marina Choi. "The Effects of Typeface on Advertising and Brand Evaluation: The
     Role of Semantic Congruence." Korean Journal of Advertising 2 (2013): 25–52. https://www.researchgatenet/
     publication/270521492_The_Effects_of_Typeface_on_Advertising_and_Brand_Evaluations_The_Role_of_
     Semantic_Congruence.

Kapadia, Amity. "Numbers Don't Lie: What a 2016 Nielsen Study Revealed about Referrals." Business2Community,
     March 12, 2016. https://www.business2community.com/marketing/numbers-dont-lie-2016-nielsen-
     study-revealed-referrals-01477256.

Khoja, Nadya. "14 Visual Content Marketing Statistics to Know for 2019." Venngage, November 15, 2018. https://
     venngage.com/blog/visual-content-marketing-statistics.

Kumparak, Greg. "A Brief History of Oculus." *TechCrunch*, March 26, 2014. https://techcrunch.com/2014/03/26/a-brief-history-of-oculus.

andy, David, and Harold Sigall. "Beauty Is Talent: Task Evaluation as a Function of the Performer's Physical Attractiveness." *Journal of Personality and Social Psychology* 29, no. 3 (1974): 299–304. https://doi.org/10.1037/h0036018.

Lewis, Peter H. "U.S. Begins Privatizing Internet's Operations." *New York Times*, October 24, 1994. https://www.nytimes.com/1994/10/24/business/us-begins-privatizing-internet-s-operations.html.

Lindgaard, Gitte, Gary Fernandes, Cathy Dudek, and J. Brown. "Attention Web Designers: You Have 50 Milliseconds to Make a Good First Impression!" *Behaviour & Information Technology* 25, no. 2 (2006): 115–126. https://doi.org/10.1080/01449290500330448.

MacArthur, Amanda. "The Real History of Twitter, in Brief." *Lifewire*, November 12, 2019. https://www.lifewire.com/history-of-twitter-3288854.

Marchant, Jo. "A Journey to the Oldest Cave Paintings in the World." *Smithsonian Magazine*, January 2016. https://www.smithsonianmag.com/history/journey-oldest-cave-paintings-world-180957685.

Mark, Joshua J. "Illuminated Manuscripts." Ancient History Encyclopedia, March 6, 2018. https://www.ancient.eu/Illuminated_Manuscripts.

Marketo. "The State of Engagement: Insights on Engagement from 2,000 Global Consumers and Marketers." 2017. https://www.marketo.com/analyst-and-other-reports/the-state-of-engagement.

McQuivey, James L. "How Video Will Take over the World." Forrester Research, Inc., June 17, 2008. https://www.forrester.com/report/How+Video+Will+Take+Over+The+World/-/E-RES44199#.

Merrill, Jeremy B., and Olivia Goldhill. "These Are the Political Ads Cambridge Analytica Designed for You." Quartz, January 10, 2020. https://qz.com/1782348/cambridge-analytica-used-these-5-political-ads-to-target-voters.

Molina, Maria D., et al. "'Fake News' Is Not Simply False Information: A Concept Explication and Taxonomy of Online Content." American Behavioral Scientist (October 14, 2019). https://doi.org/10.1177/0002764219878224.

Molla, Rani. "Mary Meeker's Most Important Trends on the Internet." *Vox*, June 11, 2019. https://www.vox.com/
recode/2019/6/11/18651010/mary-meeker-internet-trends-report-slides-2019.

Moreau, Elise. "Is Myspace Dead?" *Lifewire*, December 13, 2019. https://www.lifewire.com/is-myspace-dead-3486012.

Morning Consult. "Understanding Gen Z: How America's Largest, Most Diverse, Best-Educated, and Most Financially
Powerful Generation Will Shape the Future." Accessed January 24, 2020. https://morningconsult.com/form/gen-
z-report-download.

Morris, Errol. "Are You an Optimist or a Pessimist?" *New York Times*, July 9, 2012. https://opinionator.blogs.nytimes.
com/2012/07/09/are-you-an-optimist-or-a-pessimist.

Mozilla. "Thimble." Accessed January 28, 2020. https://foundation.mozilla.org/en/artifacts/thimble.

Mulligan, Patrick. "How Pop Chart Lab Made That Amazing Apple Infographic." *Fast Company*, May 23, 2014. https://
www.fastcompany.com/1665482/behind-the-scenes-look-the-making-of-pop-chart-labs-apple-infographic.

Nathanson, Jon. "The Economics of Product Placements." *Priceonomics*, December 4, 2013. https://priceonomics.com/
the-economics-of-product-placements.

National Museum of American History. "Magnavox Odyssey Video Game Unit, 1972." Smithsonian, accessed January 28,
2020. https://americanhistory.si.edu/collections/search/object/nmah_1302004.

Newitz, Annalee. "Printed Books Existed Nearly 600 Years before Gutenberg's Bible." *Gizmodo*, May 14, 2012. https://io9.
gizmodo.com/printed-books-existed-nearly-600-years-before-gutenberg-5910249.

Nielsen Company. "The Nielsen Total Audience Report: Q1 2019." *Radio and Television Business Report*, 2019. https://
www.rbr.com/wp-content/uploads/Q1-2019-Nielsen-Total-Audience-Report-FINAL.pdf.

Nielsen, Jakob. "How Little Do Users Read?" Nielsen Norman Group, May 5, 2008. https://www.nngroup.com/articles/
how-little-do-users-read.

———. "Photos as Web Content." Nielsen Norman Group, October 31, 2010. https://www.nngroup.com/articles/photos-
as-web-content.

Pardes, Arielle. "The WIRED Guide to Emoji." *WIRED*, February 1, 2018. https://www.wired.com/story/guide-emoji.

Playfair, William. *Commercial and Political Atlas and Statistical Breviary*. New York: Cambridge University Press, 2005.

Porzucki, Nina. "How One Man's Olympic Design Influenced Your Next Trip to the Public Restroom." PRI, February 6, 2014. https://www.pri.org/stories/2014-02-06/how-one-mans-olympic-design-influenced-your-next-trip-public-restroom.

PQ Media. "Global Branded Entertainment Marketing Forecast 2018." 2018. https://www.pqmedia.com/product/global-branded-entertainment-marketing-forecast-2018.

Project Prakash. "The Humanitarian Mission." Massachusetts Institute of Technology. Accessed January 9, 2020. http://web.mit.edu/sinhalab/prakash_humanit.html.

Project Prakash Foundation. "Project Prakash." Accessed January 9, 2020. https://www.projectprakash.org.

PwC. "A New Video World Order: What Motivates Consumers?" 2019. https://www.rbr.com/wp-content/uploads/video-consumer-motivations.pdf.

Rosenberg, Matthew, Nicholas Confessore, and Carole Cadwalladr. "How Trump Consultants Exploited the Facebook Data of Millions." *New York Times*, March 17, 2018. https://www.nytimes.com/2018/03/17/us/politics/cambridge-analytica-trump-campaign.html.

Schenkman, Bo N., and Fredrik U. Jönsson. "Aesthetics and Preferences of Web Pages." *Behaviour & Information Technology* 19, no. 5 (2000): 367–377. https://doi.org/10.1080/014492900750000063.

Semetko, Holli A., and Margaret Scammell. *The SAGE Handbook of Political Communication*. Thousand Oaks, CA: SAGE Publications Inc., 2012.

Sillence, Elizabeth, Pamela Briggs, Lesley Fishwick, and Peter Harris. "Trust and Mistrust of Online Health Sites." Conference on Human Factors in Computing Systems: Proceedings (2004): 663–670. https://doi.org/10.1145/985692.985776.

Singh, Satyendra. "Impact of Color on Marketing." *Management Decision* 44, no. 6 (July 2006): 783–789. https://doi.org/10.1108/00251740610673332.

Sklar, Robert, and David A. Cook. "History of the Motion Picture." *Encyclopædia Britannica*, accessed January 28, 2020. https://www.britannica.com/art/history-of-the-motion-picture#ref507893.

Smith, Aaron, Skye Toor, and Patrick van Kessel. "Many Turn to YouTube for Children's Content, News, How-To Lessons." Pew Research Center, November 7, 2018. https://www.pewresearch.org/internet/2018/11/07/many-turn-to-youtube-for-childrens-content-news-how-to-lessons.

Thompson, Clive. "The Surprising History of the Infographic." *Smithsonian Magazine*, July 2016. https://www.smithsonianmag.com/history/surprising-history-infographic-180959563.

Thorndike, Edward. "A Constant Error in Psychological Ratings." *Journal of Applied Psychology* 4, no. 1 (1920): 25–29. http://dx.doi.org/10.1037/h0071663.

Trafton, Anne. "In the Blink of an Eye." *MIT News*, January 16, 2014. http://news.mit.edu/2014/in-the-blink-of-an-eye-0116.

Trainer, David. "Netflix's Original Content Strategy Is Failing." Forbes, July 19, 2019. https://www.forbes.com/sites/greatspeculations/2019/07/19/netflixs-original-content-strategy-is-failing/#1efa226d3607.

Transport for London. "Harry Beck's Tube Map." Accessed January 28, 2020. https://tfl.gov.uk/corporate/about-tfl/culture-and-heritage/art-and-design/harry-becks-tube-map.

Virtual Reality Society. "History of Virtual Reality." Accessed January 28, 2020. https://www.vrs.org.uk/virtual-reality/history.html.

Whitehouse, David. "Ice Age Star Map Discovered." BBC News, August 9, 2000. http://news.bbc.co.uk/2/hi/science/nature/871930.stm.

Wilmes, Barbara, Lauren Harrington, Patty Kohler-Evans, and David Sumpter. "Coming to Our Senses: Incorporating Brain Research Findings into Classroom Instruction." *ResearchGate*, January 2008. https://www.researchgate.net/publication/234616762_Coming_to_Our_Senses_Incorporating_Brain_Research_Findings_into_Classroom_Instruction.

Wolodtschenko, Alexander, and Thomas Forner. "Prehistoric and Early Historic Maps in Europe: Conception of Cd-Atlas." *e-Perimetron* 2, no. 1 (Spring 2007): 114–116. http://www.e-perimetron.org/Vol_2_2/Wolodchenko_Forner.pdf.

Yaffa, Joshua. "The Information Sage." *Washington Monthly*, May/June 2011. https://washingtonmonthly.com/magazine/mayjune-2011/the-information-sage.

ACKNOWLEDGMENTS

To my wife: This book, let alone my company, would not have been possible without your continued support and guidance. One year after buying our home you let me risk it all on this dream, promising that you'd be happy living in a cardboard house with me as long as we were together. And through it all, that support has never faltered.

You have been a fount of wisdom through the trials and tribulations of running a business, keeping me grounded in reality at all times. From Austin to Zurich and everything in between, you have traveled the world with me as I've spoken at conferences and met with clients; all the while listening to my theories on visual communication and challenging my assumptions to ensure no stone was left unturned. Without you, I'm not sure where I would be today.

To my family: Thank you for your patience over the many years when I have had to step away to jump on a call with a client or colleague. Thank you for encouraging the opinionated side of me, because I wouldn't be here today had I not been a little too generous with my opinions of different infographics online. Thank you for encouraging me to take risks, especially when that meant moving two thousand miles away to Seattle. And thank you for always being there to listen and guide me with amazing advice.

To my Killer team: Finally, no words are enough to properly thank my team at Killer Visual Strategies! You bought into a vision centered around our core purpose to "speak visually" and have spent every day challenging yourselves to think outside the box and

expand your creative capabilities in service of our clients. Everything I shared in this book has come from lessons we have learned together.

Thanks to my executive team. You have been like partners to me as we've grown Killer in our shared vision.

To Josh Miles, Killer's president, thanks for sharing my passion for visual communication and helping me formulate the arguments laid out in this book over years of discussion and debate.

To Marli Tarbaux, Killer's COO, thanks for spending years taking work off of my plate so that I could have the time to focus on my role as CEO as well as write this book.

To Lucy Todd, Killer's CPO, you wrote the definition of visual communication shared in this book! And the processes outlined in part 3 of this book all come from years of refinement led entirely by you. Thank you!

To Charlie Holbert, Killer's CMO, thank you for spending so many years promoting our brand and establishing Killer as an industry thought leader. The opportunity to write this book resulted in large part from to your continued efforts as an amazing marketer.

To Erin McCoy, Killer's director of content marketing & PR, I can't say enough. You not only get the majority of my speaking opportunities, you have been my editor through it all. My writing has improved significantly because of you! You project managed the entire design of this book on top of doing a thorough edit. I honestly don't think this book would have come to fruition had it not been for all of your hard work!

To Andrew Willoughby, Killer's creative director, you designd the book cover and the majority of this book! Your creative vision has elevated Killer in myriad ways over the years and I will be eternally grateful!

Every designer at Killer touched this book, so a big thank you to Andrew Alimbuyuguen, Windie Chao, Taylor Doran, Jessica Eith, Megan Popovich, Blake Quackenbush, and Cole Williams.

Finally, the the rest of the Killer team not yet mentioned—Lauren Barber, Rachel Behringer, Graham Cox, Lauren Cunningham, Hilary Garman, Nic Hartmann, Lydia Nygren, Elizabeth Ossers, Abi Pollokoff, Sheridan Prince, Tim Sheehan, Eric Tra, Kameron Walsh, Eric Weinberger, and Jake Woodard —thank you!

ABOUT THE AUTHOR

Amy Balliett is the CEO and founder of the visual content marketing and communications agency, Killer Visual Strategies (formerly Killer Infographics). She owned her first company, a candy store and ice cream parlor, at the age of 17 before heading off for college. She subsequently built a successful career in SEO and marketing, and has headed up SEO at several companies. In 2009, she and her then co-founder partnered to build lead-gen-based websites, but in the fall of 2010, the business pivoted to an entirely new model: visual communication design. In the years since, she has grown Killer Visual Strategies to become the industry leader, driving visual strategy and campaigns for global brands including Microsoft, Pepsi, Adobe, Nikon, Starbucks, the National Endowment for the Arts, the United Nations, and more.

Considered an expert in her field, Amy speaks at dozens of conferences each year including SXSW, Adobe MAX, SMX, and more. She is also a regular teacher at The School of Visual Concepts, has been a guest lecturer at the University of Washington, and is a LinkedIn Learning instructor.

INDEX

Page references followed by *fig* indicate an illustration.